The BPD J
A Year in the Life

Topher Edwards
November 2012 – November 2013

Copyright © 2015 by the author. All rights reserved.

No unauthorized duplication is allowed without the express consent of the author with the exception of short quotes for the purpose of reviews, blogs, social media, or material intended to inform and educate.

First published 2015

Revised foreword 2017

Read on with caution. Many parts are disturbing and not recommended for readers under the age of 18.

You have been warned!

This book is dedicated to my family. Without your unconditional love and support, I surely would not have made it. Despite the things I may say in the following volume, I love you all.

Foreword Regarding the 'BPD Journals' Series

Since I first published this volume in 2015, it has grown into something so much more than I could have ever imagined at the time. After a slow and disheartening start, I was ready to give up and move on from my dream of being an author that inspired people both with mental illness and without. Something made me keep going. Something told me that if I pushed harder and fought for what I believed in, people would take notice – and they did.

I began seeing sales and positive reviews, so I kept writing and released my second book of the series 'Remission and Relapse'. Not long after, I had people messaging me and confiding in me, telling me they didn't feel so alone, that finally they felt like someone understood, and that maybe what they were thinking and feeling wasn't so "abnormal" after all. I also had people without any mental illness tell me that reading my books gave them a whole new perspective. They became educated and through that they began to understand what people like me, what millions of people, go through every day of their lives.

This fuelled me to continue on, as a mental health activist first and an author second. As I near completion of my third book I realize how different each volume is in the message it sends, in the mental state I am in during the span of time each one covers. Yet I also realize how consistent they are in that I am always fighting an unseen force in my head, always trying to find a positive message to send, even at my darkest times, and when I can't find one you can bet there is a random late-night rant coming.

It has been humbling and so difficult, draining and so exciting, frustrating and so goddamn rewarding to be able to put my story out there. I have to say the best part is when I see a message from a reader telling me their story and saying it was my writing that gave them the courage to speak up. You are never alone, so keep fighting – because mental illness will not stop fighting you.

Preface

For years I have suffered from mental illness. Ever since the symptoms started, I struggled to understand what was happening to me and why. After countless visits with psychologists, psychiatrists, counsellors, and general physicians, I was still lost. The plethora of medications that were prescribed to me only worked to mask some of the symptoms. They were a Band-Aid on an endlessly bleeding wound that simply would not heal. It wasn't until three years into the worst of it that I was given a diagnosis that made sense – borderline personality disorder with co-morbid major depressive disorder and generalized anxiety disorder. At the time, the diagnosis made clear what was so foggy. It helped me understand what was going on, but gave no insight as to why or what to do.

Despite the diagnosis, nothing improved. I resented the labels that were put on me and lashed out against a medical system that I felt was failing me. My head was a mess and I felt that I had no way to empty it, no one to talk to that would understand what I was going through. In 2009, during the early stages of my illness, I was still attending university. That was when I began journaling. It began as a way to put my racing thoughts onto paper; as an attempt to figure out why I felt the way I did. As time went on and my condition worsened, it became an escape. It was a 'safe' way to vent and put order to the chaos. Four notebooks currently sit in my drawer, full of the scribblings of someone in a lot of pain, both physically and psychologically. Over 700 pages chronicling my descent into near madness, which will (hopefully) never see the light of day. Writing in them was my own form of therapy, but I ran the constant risk of losing myself in those pages. My deepest secrets and darkest thoughts are written down, and even now seem to hold an energy – like they are haunted by the ghost of who I was.

On top of the written journals, I kept one online as well. Unless someone accidentally stumbled upon the Live Journal page, I believe those entries are just as unseen as those in my drawer. Starting November 2012 and ending a year later, I poured my soul into those posts. Every fucked up thing I did, every depraved thought, and every twisted dream or fantasy I had, went into the journal. It is amazing how from one day to the next I seem to shift, to change my views, my moods, and my feeling towards people or things. There, I suppose, is the typical instability of someone with BPD. Now, over two years since my last post, I have collected them into these pages, in order, with no edits and nothing censored or omitted.

It has been a long time since I have read those posts, and frankly, they scare the shit out of me. Not to say I have completely recovered from my illness (and probably never will), but I have made a LOT of progress since those days. Those days I would sit at my computer, drugged out, bleeding from self-inflicted cuts, typing away; perhaps hoping someone would in fact stumble upon my journal and give me the help I needed. It is still unclear to me why, even now, I preserve these posts. They remind me of the darkest time of my life, and maybe therein lies the answer – that darkness is the past.

Those who may read this will be shocked, sickened, confused, saddened, and surprised I am even alive at all today. I like to believe that what I went through made me stronger, as cliché as it sounds. Over the years I have learned to manage my symptoms without pharmaceuticals (save for a light sleeping pill) and lead a life that I am proud of. Maybe someone in a similar situation can read these words and see through the horrors to the real message – mental illness is not a death sentence. You can get through things that seem impossible at the time. It won't be easy, it won't happen overnight, and it will leave you with scars both inside and out that will never heal; but you will be alive. I went through Hell, but came back. I faced my Demons and won. For the time being I am managing quite well, especially when compared to the year these posts were written. That is not to say that from here on it is smooth sailing. I am well aware of the fact that this is a life-long battle and that the Demons are never completely gone, but I am also aware of the strength I now have to face them.

So without further ado, here it is. Read on with the warning that much of what follows is disturbing, to say the least. I am not proud of a lot of what I wrote during that year, but I can say that it was all the truth. I wrote all of this for myself, so why lie? Hopefully the take-away from all of this is that you gain a better understanding of mental illness. The stigma still exists today, but I am not ashamed. My case is unique, as is each and every one. Read with an open mind and try to look deeper than the words on the page.

- XV

An Introduction
November 9th, 2012

This is not an optimistic journal. You will not find happiness here, only pain. Pain is real. Pain is physical and pain is psychological. You will not agree with my entries, you will probably not like them. But they are real, they are true, and they are shocking. You will think about why someone would do the things I do, why I don't behave like society says to. The answer is simple: I'm sick. And unlike a large majority of the population, I embrace the fact that inside all of us is a monster waiting to be set free; to escape and set fire to a world ignorant to not only it's existence, but it's importance. Embracing the Dark part of my being has been both painful and enlightening. As you read more posts, you will see that ignorance is anything but bliss. That even though someone may look human, may look happy, that inside they are shattered beyond repair. So I have warned you. This is not a cry for help. I don't want it. This is not cliché, this is my life. If you take anything at all from reading this, I hope that you will open your mind and stop fearing the evil inside all of us.

- XV

Myself?
November 9th, 2012

My name is irrelevant. You will know me only as XV. Who am I really? According to "medical professionals", my labels are countless (and I do not disagree with all of them). I am depressed, I have Borderline Personality Disorder, I self-mutilate, I am an addict, insomniac, shut-in, and most of all a realist. I will not sugar-coat this for your benefit.

Having a mental illness doesn't make you who you are, but after a while, you begin to embrace it; embrace the stigma attached to your diagnosis. You discover things about yourself that most people would not believe. You see things others would shit their pants over. That is what separates you from me. I see all of myself, the good and the bad. The "normal" and the "abnormal". The person and the monster. It's that duality that defines us, and focusing on, or ignoring one part, makes us mechanical. It makes us blind and ignorant. You most likely do not agree. I do not care. This is what I have learned of myself over years of battling the dark thoughts, twisted dreams, and (for lack of a better word) the bloodlust. It was not until I stopped battling, and began to explore, that who I am as a person began to become clear. I am not saying people should act upon the bad, or the good, or both. That is a whole other ethical debate I do not care to get into. What each person does with the knowledge of who they are is what makes them who they are.

So who am I? I am an amalgamation of my thoughts, actions, feelings, dreams, and desires. I am unique in the sense that what I may see as just, others may see as horrific. What others would say is wrong, I may think is right. Ethics have very little to do with who you are once you crack open the shell and explore the chewy centre of yourself. Mine has showed me that, in my life, chaos is a large part of who I am. Creating chaos in relationships, internal chaos, and enjoying chaos even if I am not involved. Others may see chaos and try to bring order. Others may whip out the video camera. Others may enjoy it as much as I do, but may not accept that.

Exploring who you truly are, underneath the layers of shit laid upon you by societal "norms", expectations, ignorance, or whatever the case may be, is an excitingly frightening experience. You may not like what you find. You may like it, maybe too much. You may see nothing. That is what separates us. That is what makes us unique, but unique is not always a positive thing. It is what you make it. We make villains and martyrs out of people every day, but who is to say what makes a villain or a martyr?

- XV

On Letting Go
November 10th, 2012

In my experience, letting go of the people you were once close to is one of the most difficult things to do. When your sickness and actions drive everyone away, it throws you even deeper into self-destruct mode. As I have said in previous entries, my relationships become chaotic and eventually blow up, leaving irreparable damage to both people. I know that when they move on, mostly because I push them away with my words or actions, I stay in the same place. To this day there are countless people that have erased me from their lives. Whether it is justified or not is irrelevant. How you cope with the loss is what matters.

Most of the time I lack closure; a reason. Without closure, you are perpetually haunted by the separation. Even if the reason is obvious, there is no easy way to move on, despite what people say. I have lost enough to know that when people say "You are better off" or "Just move on", they do not understand. Most of the pain comes not from the separation itself, but from the chaos created internally. Psychological warfare is the worst there is. Feeling hopeless, worthless, discarded, empty, guilty, etc. wears away at you until there is little left inside. I've found this void makes it nearly impossible to trust new people, to create new relationships, or as I said, to let go of the past.

The past is vital to who you are as a person in the present. It is a common thing to hear that one should move on or forget the past, but without the past, what are you now? I feel that both my successes and mistakes over the last 22 years have moulded me into who I am today. It does not take an expert to see that some people, myself included, tend to let their mistakes define them more so than their accomplishments. Even after years, I am still haunted by mistakes I have made, people I have lost, and things I should have done differently.

Maybe there is no such thing as "letting go". Maybe we are better off remembering the good AND the bad, and realizing that without both, we would not be who we are today. Granted, the past has caused chaos in my life I never thought possible, but embracing it gives it less power to eat away at who you are.

- XV

The Self-Abuse Paradox
November 10th, 2012

When one thinks of self-harm, they think of people cutting their wrists, assumingly for attention. What they do not think of is that there are several types of self-abuse, and several reasons for doing so. Self-harm is not limited to the stereotypical wrist-cutting, but can include everything from drug abuse, to anorexia, to the extreme of auto-castration. As varied as the methods are, so are the reasons. Sure, some see it as a cry for help, some enjoy the pain, some feel worthless. Here is my story.

My body is covered in scars, varying in age and intensity. When I cut, it is usually in a place people cannot see. The stigma of self-harm has been warped to the extent that it is often associated with suicide. Though often it is true, not all self-harm behaviour has suicidal intentions. Cutting does several things for me, physically and psychologically. The pain inflicted on one's self can remind them that they are still human, capable of feeling and bleeding. The paradox comes when people say "Why cause yourself pain if you are already in pain?". Valid, but it is not so black and white. Cutting allows you to control the pain, which I have found to be a psychological release. Sometimes, the reason for cutting is unclear. Personally I have had "black-out" phases where before I realize what I am doing, the blood is already dripping. One incident left me with 30 stitches and scars that will never go away. I have had countless people make comments on the scars lining my arms, some sympathetic, some stem from ignorance.

Either way, I am not ashamed of my scars. They are a part of me, and continues to be a release for me.

As for drug abuse, it can range from reckless use of street drugs to overdosing on Tylenol, both of which I have experienced. It is no secret that street drugs are not good for your body, hence the self-abuse paradigm. Drugs are often used to escape the shitty realities of the world the user lives in. I've found it to be quite effective, but I digress. In terms of self-harm involving drugs, the end-game (for me anyway) is self-destruction. Over time your body weakens as the poisons take over. Due to overuse of Tylenol and other medications, I now need to get weekly blood tests to ensure my liver is still functioning (which, according to recent tests, it is not doing so well). This comes as a result of years of abuse and reckless consumption, combined with a disregard for my personal health. Drugs used as an escape is for a whole other post.

The other self-harm methods I mentioned, I have no experience with, so.... no comment. Essentially self-harm is a seriously misunderstood concept. People all cope with events differently, and most are able to not harm themselves in the process. But for those of us that see no other way of coping, it makes perfect sense.

- XV

Self-Esteem... Or Lack There-of
November 11th, 2012

I've noticed over my last posts that despite being honest, I have still censored myself to some extent. While it is not my intention to pour out my darkest secrets here, I need to be less "Wikipedia-ish" and more Me.

On that note, I've decided self-esteem is a great topic to pull the veil back with. It is no secret that everyone has qualities they dislike about themselves, but that is just human nature. Your self-esteem can become so low that it is practically non-existent. It is a vicious cycle brought on by not only how you view yourself, but by your idea of how others perceive you. The latter can be the most damaging. I know that from experience. When people I cared about, and thought cared about me, left me, it was a huge shot to my self-worth. My usual way of coping is to take it out on myself (probably so i do not take it out on others). I dive into drugs, cutting, and isolation. I honestly feel that if I were to bottle up my rage, and not take it out on myself, I would be a ticking time-bomb for others. I'd rather cut myself than someone else.

I will not tell you that having low self-esteem is caused by yourself or others. I will not say that it is not true. We are all ugly in some way. I will not give some inspirational speech about loving yourself because frankly, I'd be a fucking hypocrite. Feeling worthless has defined me in a way, and defines how I treat my body. The scars really prove that.

- XV

Labels Are For Soup Cans... And The Mentally Ill
November 15th, 2012

No matter who you are, what you believe in, what illness you have, or whatever the case may be, you will be labelled. You can be a jock, a goth, depressed, manic, sane, insane, rich, poor, gay, straight... The list is endless. We like to think that we are the shit and have eradicated labelling. But to be honest, we cannot function without them. Someone has to be something. Labels can be helpful, or they can be detrimental. As for me, my labels are all quite shitty. Whether the labels are accurate or not is irrelevant. I am mentally ill, I am an addict, I am a loner, an asshole... Again, my list seems endless.

Labels help people put others into categories, thus helping them be able to understand and deal with that type of person. When I go into my doctor's office, he has me labelled. I am not saying they are inaccurate, but they do change how he treats me as a patient. He knows that when I go in, he is dealing with my labels, not me as a person. Sure, who can blame him, or anyone else for that matter? I am sure that labels are essential and aid people in navigating through social situations. How people act on them is a whole different story. I am used to getting the "Fuck you" from people because of the person I am. I have accepted that most, if not all of my labels are accurate, but the stigma has been more damaging than anything. Of course I do not have the benefit of being labelled as "the rich guy" or "the mentally stable guy", so as we all do, I adapt. Some people let labels and the stigma attached break them down. I, however, have learned to embrace it. Yeah, I am pretty fucked up in the head... So what? If labelling makes it easier for you to deal with me, then by all means, label away!

Underlying the basic concept of stigma is a never-ending supply of ignorance. It is easier to label than it is to label AND understand exactly what that label means. Why look any further than the label? It clearly tells you everything you need to know! Sarcasm. They need a font for that. The point is, people tend to take the path of least resistance when dealing with others. Unfortunately, the damage has been done. Good work! This is a sad reality that we are in. Most choose to be passive or deny, but I accept them with open arms. I am insane. Be afraid.

- XV

A Taste Of The "Ultraviolence"
November 15th, 2012

Ultraviolence is a term used by Alex in the novel/film "A Clockwork Orange". Most of that movie uses slang far beyond my comprehension, but that word stuck with me. Ultraviolence refers to the use of excessive or unjustified force. Since the word was first used by the author Anthony Burgess, it has become something much more.

Violence is a part of nature, human or otherwise. When the novel came out years ago, it was shocking and obscene... Ultraviolent. By today's standards it is not nearly as shocking. We have become desensitized to violence, mostly by the media, and yes, movies, video games, etc. The most violence is seen in the news media. Murders, rapes, bombings, chaos... All televised and closed-captioned so we see everything. How many times did they show the plane smashing into the World Trade Centre, over and over? Close-ups of people desperately jumping over a hundred stories to their deaths, burnt and mangled corpses. When the Columbine Massacre happened, more focus was put on Dylan Kleibold and Eric Harris (the shooters) than the victims. We all know the names of the shooters, but most of us would be hard-pressed to name a victim.

Movies, such as the "Saw" series, shows unimaginable gore, attracting millions of viewers, each installment trying to be gorier than the last. I can go on, but I think the point has been made. Society would much rather watch a shooting or videos from the Middle East than news about a local business opening, for example. We are fascinated by violence, and the funniest (or most depressing) thing is, we all deny it. We even go as far as to alienate those that are openly violent. One of the biggest paradoxes is that a citizen is unable to kill someone who breaks into their home, yet soldiers are able to kill thousands of innocent civilians and get away with it. "Oops..". Enough about that.

Personally, I find violence fascinating. It says a lot about a person, seeing them act or react to violence. If the world burned I would not lose any sleep, and that is based on my pessimistic, but accurate, view that we fucking deserve it. I'd be lying if I said that I thought violence was pointless and negative. Sometimes violence is the only solution, and our instincts tell us "YES", while society tells us "NO". What are we supposed to believe?

My history with violence, even to the extent of Ultraviolence, is centered around my abuse of my body. Over 40 stitches from cutting, scars lining my arms like rumble strips, not to mention the violence that I cannot see going on inside my body as I bombard it with poisons and drugs. In fact, a particularly violent dream I had 4 years ago (and made the mistake of posting on here, trusting someone to understand) ended up landing me in jail. The amount of detail and violence scared the shit out of everyone who read the dream, but no one asked how it affected me. All they saw was a deranged mind; a threat to the public. Now honestly tell me you have never had a violent dream, a sexual dream, or maybe it was not a dream... Maybe you caught yourself wondering what it would be like to take a life. I know I have.

Now before I get arrested again for speaking freely and honestly, I should wrap this up. All I am saying is firstly that we are numb to violence due to overexposure. Secondly, we deny and hide our own violent nature (for the most part) because we are taught to be afraid of it. Lastly, we are all violent by nature. Embrace it. Introduce a little chaos into your life. You may just like what you find out about yourself.

- XV

Life Is A Sick, Sick Game
November 15th, 2012

I will not burst into a My Chemical Romance song, but I think my subject for this post is accurate. I will not even get into that Higher-Power bullshit. For some people, myself included, life is a sick fucking game. It toys with you, a cock-teaser that only ever blue-balls you. I am miserable beyond comprehension, and all attempts to fix that have failed miserably. I am still haunted by baggage from the past, and it weighs me down until I get stuck at rock bottom. I hate especially when people are fucking stupid enough to say "People have it worse sometimes, and they get through it. So can you." Really? Are you that ignorant to assume we are all cut from the same cloth? That how each person copes and reacts is exactly the same? Well I am truly sorry you are an idiot. Yeah, people have had worse things happen and have overcame huge obstacles. The simple fact is: I am NOT them!!!

What might be a drop in the ocean to someone could be a tidal wave to me. I take things personally, I internalize and take things out on myself. As for how I cope? While if you have read my last posts, you know I have a tendency to inflict pain on myself, whether because I think I deserve it, or because it comforts me, or maybe just because I like it. For the last 4 years I have been dealt hand after hand of shitty cards, each one adding to the chaos I experience daily. I do not want pity, that is just sad. I want understanding. I have troubles letting go, the way I cope with negative things is far from the social "norm" (fuck I hate that word), and I have fallen into a vicious cycle of perpetual pain and suffering. I have let the pain overtake, and hence the reason I am stuck where I am now. A good way to explain it is using the title of a Marilyn Manson song: I Have To Look Up Just To See Hell. That is pretty fucking far down.

But I am a "suffer in silence" type, I hold everything in. It is really hard to be 100% honest and accurate on an online journal, because frankly, there are things you would certainly not want to know. I am sick of the pain, sick of the repetition, sick of the insomnia, and sick of people telling me that I just need to get through it. Really now, Herr Dokterr? Thanks for the free advice, but I would much rather introduce your face to a brick wall than begin to explain my situation to someone who has the intelligence of said brick wall. Suffering is as much a part of me as the blood in my veins. I accept that, so why don't you?

- XV

Fuck You
November 20th, 2012

I am so sick and fucking tired of people categorizing me into these neat little categories that make it easier for them to deal with their own shit. I may be drunk at this moment, but I have just had an eye-opening experience when some cocksucker decided that I am an attention seeker. FUCK YOU. I cut because of who I am, not because I want to flaunt it. I do not wish this pain upon anyone, let alone myself. But it is a necessary part of my life. I cut so that I do not take my anger out on others. I bleed so that others do not have to. I am glad to do that. But the truth is that I do not do it for recognition or attention. I do it to punish myself for the monster I am. Fuck the ignorant that believe that they are all good. Duality is a fact of life. We are just as capable of being serial killers as we are saints.

FUCK YOU, COCKSUCKER!!!!

- XV

Filling the Void
November 25th, 2012

When you give yourself to someone else, you hand them the ability to destroy you as well. I can feel the hole in my chest, the void where a heart once beat. When she left, I lost what humanity I had left. Call me weak, I am. Words do not seem to mean anything, even actions fall upon blind eyes. You can know someone for 14 years and realize (to fault of your own as well) that when they say "Forever", it is just empty words. Through the good and the bad, the person you gave yourself to should be there. Like I said, words mean nothing, actions mean a little bit more, but keeping your word and trusting is far more important.

I have learned to accept that I have made several mistakes, but sadly realization changes nothing. If anything, it gives you a stronger understanding of who you really are and why the people you loved (and apparently loved you too) ran away. Sometimes life gets too hard to handle. You watch someone you love slipping into a world of pain and misery. Doing drugs to numb, distancing just enough that you are not pulled down with them... I fucked up. I really did. But the very principles by which we (you) live by are ignored. A hypocritical paradox, fight or flight. Flight is so much easier, so why not?

Maybe she realized I was already too far gone, too damaged to repair despite her best efforts. You cannot change the things you have done or said, but you do have **some** control over what you do next. That is a true measure of who you are. I have problems letting go of people and events of my past, and some need to be let go. Although the hole in my chest is rotting and widening with each day, each drink, each cigarette, each drug, and each sleepless night, I still have some hope that the evil has not taken over so much that she cannot stand to see me. When I stay in my old room at my Mother's place, I feel as if it is haunted, like all the time her and I spent there has left an entity there.

The void left by her leaving, as well as others, will never go away. It is as much a part of me as the blood in my veins. I have tried to fill that void, but no matter what I do, it is there... burning into me as I hopelessly pump my body full of drugs to numb the agony. My body is a pretty accurate reflection of what I feel like inside. Scarred, broken, weak... I do not think I am asking too much. I just need that light back in my life before the darkness fully takes control.

- XV

And My Heart Was A Hand-Grenade
November 25th, 2012

*"I kill myself in small amounts
In each relationship it's not about love.
Just another funeral and
Just another girl left in tears."*

- Marilyn Manson "They Said That Hell's Not Hot"

*"It's not like I made myself a list
Of new and different ways to murder your heart
I'm just painting that's still wet,
If you touch me I'll be smeared
You'll be stained,
Stained for the rest of your life."*

- Marilyn Manson "Leave A Scar"

Those two quotes have had the greatest impact on me, especially in understanding my self-destruction, as well as my (un)intentional destruction of those around me. I have hurt so many people, broken so many hearts that my own has dissolved into nothing. Maybe I did not love some of them like I thought I did. Maybe it was not necessarily about love, maybe it was about not wanting to be alone. Or maybe it stems from something deeper and darker inside. As the lyrics say, I do not intentionally blow up and destroy relationships and people. But I do have to take responsibility for the damage I leave behind. I am a painting that is still wet, meaning maybe I am not ready for "love" or a relationship. Anyone I have tried to be with has smeared me, and will be stained for the rest of their lives.

On the other hand, I do know that I have loved at least one girl I was with. I have for over a decade. The problem is that no one wants to sit around and watch as I dig myself deeper into Hell. I do not blame them. I am fucked up in several ways, ways beyond repair. I feel undeserving of what I want with her, I feel it is selfish because I know that being with her would be, and has been, the only light in my life. But for her, what do I give back? I would like to think I could do the same that she does for me, or make her feel like how she makes me, but I have come to realize I am far too gone. I have no heart to give, no happiness to share, no future to look forward to.

So, as Darwin says, only the strongest survive. I am fucking weak... pathetic, even. Naive, black-and-white, cynical, depressed, addicted... but I am not here to please anymore. I will not be the poster boy for misery. When she left, she took all I had left with her. So what am I now?

"There is an idea of me, some kind of abstraction.
But there is no real me, only an entity; something illusory.
And though I can hide my cold gaze, and you can shake my hand, and feel flesh gripping yours, and maybe you can even sense our lifestyles are comparable... I simply am not there."
   - Partick Bateman, American Psycho

That's me... an entity. Invisible to most, simply empty and abstract. I am a fucking ghost. **That** is what I am now.

Prove me wrong, fuckers.

- XV

"Just A Few Slices..."
November 27th, 2012

I had some really fucked up dreams last night. Well, more than usual. One of the wonderful side-effects of a medication I am on. I was at my doctor's office, for some reason, and he was making "Just a few slices up the arm." He began to make a large cut up the length of my forearm. "This should fix your problem.", he was saying a little too calmly. He did the same to the other arm and let the blood flow for a while before stitching both cuts up. The next parts are a little fuzzy but I remember myself and others pulling at the stitching as I wandered around an empty hospital. Then suddenly I was at my Dad's old house. We were in the kitchen, and a skunk runs inside. As I am trying to get it out the door without being sprayed, I discover why it is running. A huge wolf was outside. Its teeth were actually long, grotesque knives, stained with blood. Its eyes were a deep black. It lunged at me, but I got the door closed in time. I ran around the house locking doors and windows. I found my dad and told him what happened. We drove around the property hunting this thing down with rifles, and the last thing I remember was the wolf-thing tearing at my neck.

I woke up sweating and breathing hard. It felt so real, I expected to see the bed covered in blood. But I checked my forearms and felt my neck, and after a few minutes I was brought back to reality. Maybe I am just watching too many sci-fi and horror movies, but all I know is that I wake up more exhausted and fucked up then when I went to bed. I have given up on trying to decode these dreams. They make no sense, and the current "art" of dream interpretation is a load of bullshit. I just have to accept them as part of my "life".

- XV

I Don't Like the Drugs, But the Drugs Like Me
November 28th, 2012

Actually, who am I kidding, the feeling is mutual. I have decided to try to decode why I use drugs as an escape, but then it became painfully obvious... It's an escape. For however long that drug lasts, you do not have to feel like a bag of shit. You can forget all the bullshit that is eating away at your mind. Physically, you do not feel much at all. The ethical question of drugs has no place here, and will not be explored. What I will say is that drugs have been the worst and the best thing for me. They have driven me to psychosis, damaged my body and mind, caused a lot of chaos within myself and my family and friends. At the same time, they have given me the break I needed from the shit-storm I call my life. Some people can cope without turning to drugs. Well, then good for you, this blog is not meant for you. From pot to blow, MDMA to Oxycontin, Xanax to Adderall, I have pretty much tried it all.

Painkillers were my drug of choice for quite a while. The reason is self-explanatory... it killed the pain. Then cocaine became my thing, and an endless amount of ecstasy and various pharmaceuticals followed soon after. I smoked pot for the first time when I was 12. Grade 6. From there I was able to control my use (along with alcohol) throughout most of high school. It was not until the middle of Grade 12 that I discovered the wonders of narcotics. I went from Tylenol 3 to morphine pretty fast, to the point I was constantly puking, shaking, and not eating. It calmed down a bit when I began University. There I would smoke the odd joint, maybe do some amphetamines to aid in my studying, and sometimes the odd opiate. It was not until I fell mentally ill and left University that drugs became a large part of my life.

I will not go into all the boring details, but I will say this. I have never been so high, or so low, as when I am using. It is interesting to think of how much money I have spent on chasing that high. The high that got me through when she left, when the others did too, when my mind-numbing job was destroying me, that has caused me to be more numb than I ever imagined; that high is still something I chase, and long for... and always will. In fact, right now, I am using. Against my better judgement (or lack thereof) I made that call, and here I am, shaking, sweating, numb, care-free, and completely not caring what the consequences will be.

I do not advocate the use of drugs, that is a decision each person must make for themselves. I do, however, hate the stigma surrounding it. I have discovered more about myself after a line of coke than with any shrink. This is MY story, MY experiences, MY opinions, and ultimately MY choice. I do not lose any sleep over those that look down their noses at me. We are all weak. What your weakness is happens to be a whole different story.

"There's a hole in our soul that we fill with dope. And we're feeling fine."
  - Marilyn Manson - I Don't Like The Drugs (But The Drugs Like Me)

- XV

On A Roll
November 29th, 2012

Well, I did not sleep last night. I used to do that for days in a row, you know, when I was young and crazy. But being 22... Really takes its toll. Today I feel great, despite my lack of sleep. Why? I will give you a hint... Read my last post.

I am starting to reconnect with some old friends. I have isolated myself for so long, I forget what to do in a social situation. Anyway, this could be a good step forward for my mental health, or it can blow up and justify my cynical views of people. I like to anticipate both scenarios.

Generally, my clean bill of health (liver function) has given me another chance. I think it is chance number 115. Part of me feels like I cheated death, again, but I know eventually I will lose the game of chicken I play with my life.

- XV

Losing
December 1st, 2012

Did I really have a chance in the first place? I am responsible for the things I did, but circumstance and illness is beyond anyone's control. Feeling hopeless eats away at you from the inside out. You fall into a cycle of destruction and chaos, and reality slips away. Days mean nothing, sleep is impossible, and you feel like you have failed to hold on to one of the most important things in your life. We spent years and years on a rollercoaster ride through pain and happiness, but eventually the ride gets to be too much and stops.

I will never forgive myself for what I did to end up here, and I do not care if it kills me. I feel dead already. Purgatory is worse than Hell. Today is not going to be a good day for me, but it will be for her. I am happy that she is happy, but I cannot help but feel a burning pain inside my chest that reminds me of what, and who, I have lost. Where I go from here does not matter to me. I have accepted my place in the universe, and I will just sit back and let life fuck me and toss me aside... like a leper.

- XV

449,686,566 Seconds (And Counting)
December 2nd, 2012

449,686,566 seconds... about 5,205 days... 743.5 weeks... 171 months... 14 years...

It feels like forever since Grade 3. I was young and naive, but what I did know is that I wanted her in my life. As a friend, as a listener, as a girlfriend, as everything. Now, however, we might as well be strangers. People keep telling me to get over it, to move on, to let it go. I cannot throw away about 63.6363% of my life because someone says "Move on". Putting this into numbers and percentages may be my way of making this easier to handle, but nothing can really make this any easier.

It is the not getting to say goodbye that makes this feel like I am mourning a death, and in a way I am. Writing about it will not change her or my actions in the past, present, and probably future. I just wish that 14 years created a stronger bond that was much harder to break. How can I ask her to forgive me if I cannot forgive myself?

- XV

Reality vs. Nightmares
December 4th, 2012

The last few weeks have really taken its toll on me, mentally and physically. The details are irrelevant, other than what glimpses I have given you over the last posts. The fact is I cannot eat, I cannot sleep, I cannot stop the shakes, and to be honest it is harder every day to separate the nightmares I have from my "real" life. I have to convince myself that the nightmare was not real, even though it feels more and more real. I am my own biggest tormentor. My unconscious spilling into my conscious is turning me into a nervous, paranoid wreck. The plethora of pills I am given have stopped working. Even double my dose does nothing to stop the shakes, nothing to help me sleep, and nothing to improve my mood. It is safe to say I am more than hopeless. Having tried over 30 different medications, I know that the possibility of finding one that works is getting lower and lower every day. I felt more stable on cocaine... on ecstasy... on the narcotics. They are the only thing that works, and the only thing I cannot have.

I feel myself unravelling. I can barely type these words I am shaking so much. My dad is bitching over my addiction, when he is an alcoholic. He treats me like a fucking two year old. I finally stood up and said "Go fuck yourself." All I really have is my Mom, my Aunt, and my Brother. Without them I would certainly be dead. I do not know what will happen if this keeps going the way it is. I am weaker every day and I cannot hold out much longer. Eventually I am going to snap, and either put myself in the hospital again... or someone else.

So here I sit, at yet another cross-roads. One wrong turn and I will set the world on fire. My savage will to live is disappearing faster than She did. I have felt psychosis before, and to tell you the truth, this feeling is far too similar. Hold on tight.

"Spread me open,
Sticking to my pointy ribs
Are all your infants in abortion cribs
I was born into this
Everything turns to shit
The boy that you loved is the man that you fear
Pray until your number,
Asleep from all your pain,
Your apple has been rotting
Tomorrow's turned up dead"
- 'Man That You Fear' - Marilyn Manson

- XV

End of an Era
December 5th, 2012

This is the end, the end of an era wrought with love, pain, destruction, lows, highs, and mistakes. Though this era ends, a new one begins. This is not through choice. This is a necessity. The old me has transformed. You will like this me even less, and less as I go along. Fuck the weakness I have let bring me to my knees. Fuck the ignorant who tell me what my life should be. Fuck trying to make you happy. It has got me nowhere.

Ladies and Gentlemen, the new me, the new era, is not for your benefit. It will not appeal to you. Though many of you created this, I alone became this way. If it is not to your liking, stall your words and hold your breath. As you turn blue I will become something more and something less at the same time. The shadows have become my refuge from the violent shit-storm I lived in. Not anymore. Not now. Now, I will not fear the thoughts, the compulsions, the desires, nor the shadows. The voice that once screamed NO, that once held me back, has been stifled. I have bound and gagged the "Angel" on my shoulder and made room for the Demons.

This is no lie, no literary tale. This is truth, and most of you do not like the truth. Maybe it is because the truth is too frightening. You would rather hide behind some delusion you are content, incapable of the things I have done and will do. That is a lie. That is an illusion.

This, however, is my truth. Get ready, I warn them, things are going to get messy.

- XV

It's What I Tell Myself to Make the Thoughts Okay
December 9th, 2012

Anyone with a mental illness can tell you that thoughts can become your worst enemy, as well as your only salvation. Sometimes it is like looking into the eyes of the Devil himself. A blackness encompassing your world. Society tells you to be afraid of the Darkness, be very afraid. Well fuck that. Embracing the Darkness is embracing another part of yourself. Duality is the theme here. Anyone is capable of being a saint just as much as they are capable of being a serial killer. But that cannot be right, so we are told to ignore it. It is a question of nature vs. nurture. The good twin and the evil twin. We are all monsters, capable of horrific acts of violence and cruelty, but for you optimists out there, we are all capable of acts of generosity and love. The fact is however, we live in a world saturated with violence, pain, and misery. Positivity is a rare commodity, and is getting more and more scarce by the day.

Maybe duality is my way of telling myself that what I see in my head is okay. Break something I do not understand down into science. All I know in the end is what I see and feel, and you would not like to see into my head.

- XV

Run
December 11th, 2012

I have spent the last 3 years watching people run away from me, from who I have become. I do not blame them. If I could run, I would too. I am not the same person as I was 3 years ago, when I was first diagnosed. The diagnosis, however, is irrelevant to me. I will not sugar-coat my experiences for your benefit, I will not ease into the pain, and I will not expect you to stick around. This is not some attempt to alienate myself, to boast of my misery. This is bone-hard medical fact. I refuse to censor myself so that you can believe that there is still good inside, I would not expect you to be that naive. I know why you run. You run because the only thing more frightening than reality is facing it. So you can run and hide, cower in the shadows and tell yourself that everything will be okay. It will not. I am done ignoring the truth. Done with the excuses and the false reasons for why I am who I am. You made your choice, and so have I. I have decided not to bathe myself in your ignorance and hypocrisy, and you have decided that you should run instead of trying to understand. Suit yourself. Live in your perfect world that threw me away, encase yourself in Good, and pretend that Bad does not exist. I do not want to be a part of your Hate Culture, making martyrs out of the sick, giving excuses for the weak, and glorifying the strong to the point of making them deities.

So I say, with finality, I do not want you to like me. I will not beg for your attention. You have made your opinion clear, and now I have done the same. One day you will look back and remember me as the druggie, the freak, the whatever... But as long as you live, there will still be traces of me in your veins. A bad taste in your mouth constantly reminding you why you had to run. You will have that. And in the end, I will have what I want. One way or another.

- XV

T-Minus 9 Days
December 12th, 2012

Nine days until December 21st, 2012. The supposed End of the World. The Apocalypse. According to the ancient Mayans and Doomsday-Freaks alike, we only have 9 days left on this world. Will it be a great flood? Nuclear holocaust? Rogue asteroid? Aliens? Everyone has their theories, and most of them are dumb as fuck. People are already spending thousands in survival gear for the "Endtimes". Yay Capitalism!

What do I think? (Whether you care is irrelevant). I think people are obsessed with death, destruction, and chaos. They pretend to be appalled, but how many turned away when the Twin Towers went ka-boom? As Marilyn Manson says, "*The death of one is a tragedy, the death of millions is just a statistic.*" When someone is murdered, people start freaking out! But when a mass event causes thousands to die, we seem to go balls deep into it, watching every video, every death toll, every sickening detail we absorb and in some way, enjoy. Do not deny it.

Of course people are obsessed with chaos. I can relate, BPD is all about chaos, and of that, I have had plenty. I do not care if the world ends tomorrow, or 50 years from now. Either way it is uncontrollable and even if I did care enough about myself, there would still be nothing I can do to prevent it. So just accept it. You will die. Today, tomorrow, in 9 days, or 60 years. We all die in the end.

That is where it ends.

- XV

Death
December 13th, 2012

Over the past years I have done a lot to damage my body. Twice I was so close to Death, I could feel the cold surrounding me. About 6 months ago, I was filled with drugs, and void of any hope or happiness. I cut myself..deep... at least 20 times. I lost about half the blood in my body as I laid there in a pool of my blood. Eventually, something told me to call 911, and the doctor told me if I did not, I would certainly have died. Thirty stitches, and a week in the psych ward later, you would think I learned my lesson. A few months later I overdosed on narcotics. Again, I took more than enough to kill me, and once again I felt the cold air of Death. The doctors pumped me full of meds to block the damage, and told me I would likely need a new liver. Somehow, I cheated Death again.

When you begin to enter the first stages of Death, you feel light and weak. Nothing else matters, not the damage you will leave behind, not the people who will be torn apart... nothing. A sense of calm comes over you. I did not panic, I did not stop. I laid there, relaxed, and waited for the End. I guess everyone has a voice inside telling them to do the right thing. The voice was loud enough that I called for help, but my intention was to die there on my bed. Coming back from the hospital, my room looked like a crime scene. The bed was covered in dark, dried blood. A puddle at least a foot across of thick blood was on the floor next to the bed, where I had dangled my arm down to let more blood out. The knife was also bloody and stabbed into the wall. The entire room was a mess, and there was very little that did not have blood on it. That is when it really hit me, how close I came. But in my cocaine and ecstasy induced psychosis, it felt right to cut. Did I change from that experience? No.

The next time, I took enough painkillers to kill two people. It was not as calm as when I had almost bled out. I was violently sick, eventually puking blood and bile. A similar sense of euphoria came over me, but still that voice was there, causing me to call for help. Once again I failed. My liver somehow survived, and so did I.

I am not glorifying suicide, or self-harm. But you gain a new understanding of Death when you are so close to it. It is not always like in the movies where a near death experience causes you to respect life more. My actions since have proved that. I have not changed for the better. Every pill, every line of coke, every cigarette, and every shot of alcohol brings me closer to the End. As the saying goes, third time's a charm... Three strikes and you're out... We will see I guess.

- XV

The Last Hurrah?
December 16th, 2012

This weekend was all about substance, all about abuse, all about that high. Maybe it is what needed to happen if these conspiracy theorists are right about the Apocalypse. More likely, it is just me having the right amount of access, money, and cravings. Whether or not the world will end in 5 days or not does not matter to me. I already feel dead, a ghost trapped in purgatory, endless pain and emptiness. I am in my own Hell, but I do what I need to in order to take the pain away, at least for a while. That makes me an addict. So fucking what?

- XV

Mechanical Animals
December 16th, 2012

No copyright infringement intended to Mr. Manson, but I feel this is a topic everyone can relate to and has experienced.

It can be argued we need rules to survive, Anarchy is not used for a reason. But in the end not only are we all animals capable of horrific acts, but societal pressure and rules have made us no more than mechanical. Robots programmed to behave, to contribute, to act as we are expected. I say fuck that. We let a small group of rich white people decide what we can do and what we cannot, what is right and what is wrong. Take drugs for example. For decades, the government has been losing the drug war, leaving thousands of casualties in their wake. However, being high on these illegal drugs is the best I have ever felt. I could go on, but it would be like talking to a brick wall.

My point is that we are so mechanical, it is as if we are all mechanical, built to follow laws that make no sense. Come on, try a little lawlessness. Try giving Harper the finger, rob someone, hit someone in the face, I would bet my left nut that you will enjoy it more than you have been told you would.

It Should Be Easy...
December 18th, 2012

Falling asleep is one of the most natural and simple things the human body does. It is essential. So why the fuck don't the handfuls of pills I take each night work? I have tried just about every sleeping pill there is, and for some reason, none work. Maybe it's more psychological. I know that when I go to bed, my unconscious mind is free to take over. Countless disturbing, and recurring, nightmares are already burned into my mind, maybe it is more of a defense mechanism against further damage.

All I know for sure is that I am sick and fucking tired of feeling like a zombie every day because I spend the night tossing, turning, and swearing. It's a helpless feeling that is getting to be too much to handle.

- XV

Apocalypse How
December 22nd, 2012

December 21st has come and gone without incident. Maybe the worst damage is done to the "Preppers" who spend thousands on bunkers for the End of Days. Bet they are pretty fucking embarrassed.

To be honest, I stood outside having a cigarette last night and heard several loud pops and bangs. I looked over and with each bang the sky lit up. I heard several sirens and what sounded like jets flying overhead. At the time I must admit I was a little freaked out, thinking that something big was going on. But the shitty weather made it impossible to see where the bangs came from. It didn't take me long to figure out that it was most likely fireworks, and the sirens were due to the morons that decided it was a nice night for a drive.

I knew nothing was going to happen, that I would wake up today and the world would still be here. I cannot deny that I am a little let down. So much build-up for nothing. I have been Apocalyptically blue-balled. But of course, it could still happen any day. I sort of hope for a Zombie Apocalypse. I am a sort of expert in killing zombies from all the movies I have watched.

We seem to be fascinated with our own demise. Creating wild theories based on ancient people who couldn't even understand lightening seems a little fucked up. December 21st 2012 will simply go down in the books as another fear campaign (much like the Y2K bug) that was an epic failure. I shake my head at the idiots hiding in their bunkers. Scratch that, I shake my head at anyone who puts all their faith in the prophecy of a civilization that couldn't even save themselves from being wiped out.

- XV

Shoot 'Em Up
December 22nd, 2012

Once again, mankind has proven that we are not as evolved as we think, that we are much more twisted than we think, and much, much more capable of grotesque acts than we think. There is a plague called Ignorance, running rampant throughout the world. It is infecting everyone, but it is fitting that we pay the price for our own failures.

Let me start off by mentioning a few things that, from recent events, have become relevant again. Columbine, Virginia Tech, the Polytechnique Massacre. And now Sandy Hook Elementary. School shootings have been around for over a century, but now, shootings have never been so popular, so covered by media, and so twisted and abused. What happened at Sandy Hook is undeniably horrific, but also inevitable. As long as there are people, there will be people killing people. The shooters can be seen as sick fucks, mentally ill, Marilyn Manson fans, or just angry. Almost as tragic as the shootings is the news coverage. All over television the faces of the shooters, their names, and their kill count are glorified and repeated over and over. When Eric Harris and Dylan Kleibold shot up Columbine, it was their names we remember. I challenge you to think of the names of even ONE of the victims of Columbine....

Thought so. Over 13 years later, the shootings continue, more frequently than before. No matter what anti-gun protesters, religious zealots, or politicians do, people are going to die. What makes me laugh is the "quick and efficient" response to the shootings by the government. I heard one idea to solve the issue of shootings that made me both laugh uncontrollably and shake my head at the same time. This brilliant idea involved arming the teachers in schools nation-wide... Yeah. Exactly. So what would that do? I think it would teach kids that guns are necessary, and belong in schools. It would desensitize them to the idea of guns. It would bring guns into schools, giving any student access to a gun. It would entail teachers to become targets and expected heroes if a shooting occurred.

My point is, it never fails to amaze me how fucking stupid and backwards people are. There is no solution. No answer. No quick fix. Make guns illegal, you start an underground market similar to the cocaine trade. You will never pry the guns from people's hands. You will never fix their mental illnesses in time, you will never stop people from killing. It's like trying to stop a tornado using a fan. You will fail.

What happened last week is tragic, don't get me wrong. But what overall is more tragic is the continued ignorance of mankind.

- XV

Three Years Ago
December 22nd, 2012

Blood was everywhere. Snow fell lightly, and the wind did little to mask the sobs and cries of pain. In the middle of the forest, there was no one to help, nothing I could do.

I wish this was a nightmare, or something I made up in my twisted mind. But on this day, three years ago, I held her in my arms as the pills poisoned her and the blood gushed from her arms. To this day I still feel sick, and am still haunted by what happened that night. That night, even though no one died, the spark did. A piece of ourselves, and of us, died in that forest. I have spent the last three years suffering, torturing myself for the choices I made that day. It will never get easier. I showed my true monster by doing what I did. Allowing what happened to happen.

I can't even say if she is still affected by that night. I can't even guess. She has shown to be cold-hearted, but I'm sure there are still traces of that night in her veins.

I fucked up.

- XV

Temptation Is A Bitch (When You Are Weak)
December 22nd, 2012

My life is a little too cyclic for my own good right now. Every day is way too much like the last, and what I do to make the days bearable is dangerous and will eventually be my demise. I admit I have an issue. Even Hellen Keller could see that I do. The thing is, I don't really want to change... I don't know if I can, even if I wanted to. I've carved out a nice little niche here in my room, being reckless and going nowhere. With so much damage in my wake, who would want to share in a future so uncertain? How could I ask that of anyone? I can't. I won't.

It's really all too much to think about. My mind is enough of a mess already. Fuck it. Let it snow, and see what happens.

- XV

Insomnia
December 23rd, 2012

2:40 a.m.: Still awake, my own doing. Is it worth it? Probably not, but since when have I cared? Maybe there is a reason to, maybe I just need to find it.

Maybe.

- XV

Deja Vu
December 27th, 2012

Yet another day spent trembling, uncertain, anxious, and down. Take down the balloons, I do not want a pity party. It's just fact. Cold, hard, fucking fact. There are very few places, if any, left for me to turn to. I am afraid of getting close to someone because I know I would only end up breaking them as I have done to myself. But this is no way to live... This is not survival, this is empty existence. Seeing Marilyn Manson in a month is all I can look forward to, considering tomorrow, and the days after that, will only be as tedious as the last. An infinite cycle, Deja vu. I feel I have been here before. I feel I cannot leave this place, as if it has a grip on me. Maybe I do not want out anymore.

- XV

Weak
December 29th, 2012

How can something have so much power over a person? Where every minute of every day is spent thinking about it, wanting it, knowing that it will eventually destroy you. I guess I am just another one of the weak. We all have weaknesses, some more severe than others. All I know is that right or wrong, bad or good, healthy or otherwise, the cravings will never go away. At the end of each dose is the need for another, and another, and another. You can numb yourself, but eventually reality comes rushing back in a wave of despair and pain.

Now for my reality. I do not see a reason to stop, at least not one that is good enough. I know it is killing me, but I could not pretend to care if I tried. I am not sick, or in need of help... I just do not want to feel the pain anymore. I have stopped caring what people say, they can say what they want, and they can force themselves to mean it, but it will never change me. Who really cares anyways? Who am I destroying but myself? Is it **just** me that is the selfish one?

- XV

Cloud Nine
December 30th, 2012

I feel like I have sold my soul to the Devil. I feel he manipulates and controls me... sometimes. I sit here, alone, flying high, making a friend out of a toilet paper roll and post-it notes. His name is Karl.. with a K, not a C. Karl likes to sit and glare, tempting and taunting me as I give in to my temptations. It is temporary, but necessary to keep my sanity. Escaping life for a day or two makes me feel better, even if it's just for a little while.

While I give into this temptation, another one is being born. One that should not happen. One that cannot happen. One I want to happen. But if I give in, I risk failure, and I risk destroying everything.

- XV

New Year, New Fear
January 7th, 2013

Obviously for me, the New Year was brought in under a haze of various uppers and downers, with dubstep blaring in the background. Crowds of partiers under the influence of various mind-benders and mood-enhancers danced and swayed to the relentless beat. It was surreal. That really is the only way to describe that night, as well as time following.

Seeing my brother for the first time since the summer was great. He and his girlfriend seem to have found what most people will look for forever and never obtain - a healthy, stable relationship. Two words I would only use ironically to describe myself.

I did not bother to make any resolutions for the New Year... I never have, and I would only set myself up for further failure. I will not try to mind-fuck myself into believing that after years of depravity, THIS will be the year I clean up my act. The ignorant can tell themselves that they will finally drop those last few pounds, get that promotion at work, or become a better person, for everyone's sake. So fucking naive. Sure, realistically there will be people that succeed. More power to them. But I know myself, and I know what is inside. Change seems to be an impossible task, one I hold myself back from achieving. Why change? For who? To what end? If I was to even try to make a resolution, it would only be a shit-covered lie. I am not stupid enough to fool myself into doing that. Call me cynical. Fuck, I know I am cynical. But behind that cynicism is truth... realism. I know how I live my life is for the most part considered "unhealthy and wrong" by society. However, the part of me that used to give a fuck has long since been ripped from me (along with several other parts that would make me mechanical enough to fit into the world as a whole).

You would be a fucking moron to take advice from someone like me, but I will give some anyway. Do not set goals that you will not reach. Do not set goals that other people will like and accept. A goal is not always a positive ideal, a goal is simply what you want and where you want to be. I set no goals, but that is because I am simply afraid of both change and failure. Change would mean getting rid of the substances that make life bearable. No, I am not suicidal. Been there, tried that, found out fast that it is only a sign of cowardess. Anyway, I digress. No matter how much my self-destruction has fucked up my life, I still seem to consistently return to what I can only describe as my "primal" self. The part of me that craves the numb and euphoria promised by a little pill, a line of powder, or a swig of alcohol.

Is it really so bad to want to feel euphoric instead of depressed? Is it wrong to want to escape the void I have called my home for the last three years? Sure, the law and the general population say that it is in fact wrong, and illegal. Do I give a fuck? Hahahahaha... no. Should I?

Maybe. Wondering about what other people think is one less thing I give myself to worry about. I do not expect approval, or even understanding. I just expect that what I do to myself, "right" or "wrong" is ultimately my choice. Sure, you can have your say, but so can I.

The New Year will be anything but dull, I am guessing. There always seems to be some drama working its way into my life. Whether I am flying high, writing an online journal that no one reads, or being a good little robot, there are two things that will certainly never change: I do not give a fuck about the consequences of my lifestyle, and I will not change to fit into some cookie-cutter citizen for approval.

2013, bring it the fuck on.

- XV

This Addiction (And a Friendly Reminder to a Friend)
January 8th, 2013

Since before high school I have been chasing high after high, jumping from pot to coke to morphine, trying to find the perfect level of numb. Control has never been one of my strong points, and has become a constant battle for me. Sometimes I will find that perfect high. It will make the rest of my time spent in pain worth it. The problem is that next time, there is no guarantee the high will be the same. This is where all control is lost. Like a parent searching for a lost child, I scramble from shady dealer to dealer. Trying new drugs, new combinations, chemicals I cannot even pronounce, I all too seldom find that perfect high anymore. I know that this is a curse I bear, one I put on myself, one that will never break. So onwards goes the struggle between control and substance, between pain and numb, between me and myself. Looking back at the journals I have kept since November 2009, I can see my progression through this surreal world of chemical stimulation. Each year, I seem to falter more and more. I have stopped the pity-parties I used to throw for myself. It's just pathetic. I dug my own hole, and I will most certainly be buried in it. It is only a question of when, not if.

P.S. - A friendly reminder to a friend of mine that they have promised me that they will post something. Just saying.

- XV

End The Cycle
January 11th, 2013

I am at a crossroads in my life. Each potential path I could take scares me, perhaps it's the unknown. For years, my life has been centered around one thing - drugs. Can I end the cycle? From previous posts, my opinion of drugs is obvious. Why I use is maybe a bit less clear, but still there. I'll let you figure that one out. An ultimatum only sent me back to the same path. Now the game is changing. How? Well to protect certain people, as well as myself, I cannot say. I seem to be faced with the question of whether or not I can distance myself from the triggers that set me off onto a trip to Cloud 9. All I see when I look ahead is the fog of uncertainty. I know not to expect a miracle. It will not be easy. I cannot even say that I am fully ready to do what it would take to end the cycle. I cannot say that I may ever be. I live one day at a time. I cannot take on too much at once or everything seems to crumble. Can I live without this feeling?

- XV

The Day That Never Was
January 14th, 2013

Saturday was not a day for me. All it is now is a foggy estimation of what I did for 24 hours. A post-it note declaring "Any DXM is too much DXM" is all that is left from a day wiped from memory. The dissociation in itself is quite unnerving, the feeling that you have left your body and it is now on auto-pilot. Your senses are warped beyond recognition and every task seems monumental. My brain had never been so numb. As I floated beside what I could only assume was my body, I felt like I would never regain control over myself. It was a feeling of helplessness that only grew as time went on. I cannot remember the details of that day, or even the day after. It's as if they have been pulled from my brain. It was easy to get lost in whatever it was I was doing. I couldn't speak, I couldn't think, I could only watch as my body moved and my mind wandered. I'm just happy that the effects weren't permanent. Robo-tripping, as they call it, seems harmless, but it was a step beyond reality that words just cannot explain. It hold your brain hostage and injects the fear of never being free from the effects. I'm just waiting for the next stupid stunt I pull that will finally be irreversible.

- XV

Repetition
January 16th, 2013

I'm tired of every day being exactly like the last. While the answer seems simple, it isn't. There is little I can do to end the cycle, and little I can do to save myself. The things I want, the people I want in my life are unattainable. Maybe this purgatory is my punishment for the life I have lived.

- XV

I Saw a Man
January 18th, 2013

I saw a man today, picking through a garbage bin. Desperately searching for something to eat, maybe something warmer to wear. His clothes were a patchwork of salvaged materials. As I watched, he continued onto two more garbage cans. Any sense of pride or self-esteem was long gone. I could tell by his eyes. It is a frigid day today, even wearing a $250 coat, I was shivering. It was all about survival.

I was waiting for the bus as this was going on. I barely have a penny to my name, only circumstance separated this man from me. People are quick to judge and even quicker to swat these people off like flies. I heard a woman on the phone saying that the man was probably a crack head, then bursting into ignorant laughter. I shook my head. In a world so full of materialism, socio-economic gaps, and decadence, this woman assumes and asserts her place above this man on her hypothetical hierarchy. If I had even a dollar to spare, I would help. It is one of the few good things I consistently do.

What I learned from this experience was something I had always thought to be true, but was now solidified in my mind. We live in a world of arrogance and ignorance. We are so full of ourselves, oh we, saints among men. Their worth is calculated by the money in their bank and the fancy cars they drive. Why develop a caring personality when you can just buy your way through life. We are so arrogant to say that we live in a great country, where we help our fellow man, where we are educated and civilized. Where is the civility in watching a man rummage through garbage just so he doesn't starve to death as countless people have the means to help. There is far more money in this world than we can use, but it seems that the social "elite" are happy with their materialistic lives, and lose no sleep over the man picking through garbage.

What is your social status? What is it built upon? What do you think when you see people spending millions on cars, with no regard for the man picking through the garbage? What a backward fucking world we live in.

- XV

The Way I Am
January 18th, 2013

Change is constant, in every aspect of every life. Looking back on the last few years, even just the last year, I can see change. I can also see things that are too similar for my liking. If I am to become a successful member of society, achieve my "potential", change is something I will have to do a lot of. I am far from stable, school seems unlikely... I don't even know what I like anymore, and as for sobriety, well that's a whole other story I am putting off for now. Without any idea of where I want to be in five years, it's hard to start doing things to get out of this grave I have been digging for myself. These are not excuses, do not mistake them for that.

Of course I want to change (certain) things about me. Clearly, there is a large gap between where I am and where I want to be. There's an even larger gap between where I am, and where those close to me want me to be. I try not to focus on that too much. Change is inevitable, and will come. It's just a matter of when and how. I guess I am not ready to change certain things, despite their detrimental effect on my life. However, the seed of change is planted, and it is up to me to water it and care for it, and hopefully eventually things will become clearer. Hopefully my cheesy metaphors will be part of that change.

- XV

Closing the Gap
January 19th, 2013

I find the fact that yesterday's post will certainly cause some confusion after this one is read quite funny. It wasn't exactly an epiphany, it was more of a challenge. Can I actually turn things around? How fast? Will it last? I've decided to pursue school, get healthier, and try to beat this addiction. Now it must be said that I will still dabble in the world of drugs, but I've decided to push myself.

This new "era" began with waking up before noon (wow), exercising, and taking a walk. For me, that is a **huge** achievement. For others, it's just another day. Despite taking MDMA yesterday, I woke up feeling pretty good, and the exercise made me feel a bit better. At first it will be hard to get my body away from the drug-addled stasis I've lived in for years. I will be looking into part-time courses today.

Now of course there is a pretty big chance that this whole "rebirth" will crash and burn like the plane that hit the World Trade Centre, but firstly, what the hell else do I have to do? And secondly, it might not. Stay tuned. I'm sure this will be an interesting endeavor.

- XV

A New Era, Perhaps
January 21st, 2013

I am not one to get ahead of myself and make proclamations that I cannot guarantee. I have registered for a course in abnormal psychology (10 points for irony), quit smoking, and my drug use is pretty much at zero. All these changes happened suddenly, and now it becomes a game of keeping the momentum up and not slipping back into my old ways. However, I do not plan to cut anything from my life completely. I will still dabble the odd time in drugs, maybe have a smoke one day when I am drinking... But what I have started to do is something I never thought would happen anytime soon. It has made people close to me happy, and put a smile on the face of someone I care deeply about.
Now it's just time to wait and see how it goes.

- XV

Well I Never Knew... (You Were So Disposable)
January 23rd, 2013

I cringe at the number of hours I have spent in misery over you. I see now that you are nothing more than a coward, running from person to person, place to place, just to escape when things get tough. Your beliefs may have a lot to do with it, I'm guessing. Sure, a coward is also someone who covers up pain with drugs, but at least I admit it. It's probably just hard to see from way up on your fucking pedestal, looking down on us for being human. Why I spent so much time trying to get over you is beyond me, but it has become very simple. Peeling back the layers I can see how ugly you really are. I wish you nothing but misery, and I am not ashamed to say so.

- XV

Countdown to the Apocalypse
January 24th, 2013

Only five days until my life is complete. Five days until I finally see Marilyn Manson live. It's been one of only a few dreams I've ever had, and if I die the day after, I will die happy. Of course much love is sent out to the girl who made this possible. You don't know what it means to me.

While I would enjoy the show a bit more on MDMA, staying clean seems to make more sense. It's taken a heavy toll on my body already. The withdrawals are causing unrelenting pain and fatigue that are wearing me down. This concert is all that really keeps me going, and afterwards, I guess I'll have to try to find something new to get me through. I honestly do not care about my body, or the shit I put into it. If it were up to me, I'd have the mountain of coke in front of me like on Scarface. But it seems that a few people care, and I have the tendency to feel guilty over the few people who believe in me. My battle with drugs is faaarrrrr from over. It will likely never end, but taking it one day at a time makes it just a little more bearable. Until, of course, my inevitable relapse.

- XV

Fueling the Fire
January 25th, 2013

"Don't break, don't break my heart
And I won't break your heart-shaped glasses
Little girl, little girl you should close your eyes
That blue is getting me high, making me low."

- Heart-Shaped Glasses (When The Heart Guides The Hand), Marilyn Manson

"Love is a fire,
Burns down all that it sees.
Burns down everything.
Everything you think,
Burns down everything you say."

- Just A Car Crash Away, Marilyn Manson

I chose these two lyrics because of their truth and relevance in my life. Love is a fire, everyone and everything it touches will eventually go up in flames and turn to ash. These may sound like the remarks of a pessimist, but they are instead (while similar) the remarks of a realist.

Every thought, every possibility, every uncertainty slowly fuels a fire that should be extinguished before anyone can get burned (besides me). The thought of her lips, her hands; us embraced in a perfect Fuck. Vulgarity aside, it is impossible to escape the "what-ifs", and impossible to escape the longing for these possibilities to happen. I may be broken, and people should generally avoid any emotional relationship with me, but these fantasies transcend reality. They are like a drug, filling me with lust and longing. The worst part is I know how wrong it would be, and that makes me long for it more. I should just stop before I explode and take anyone with me, especially her.

- XV

Closer
January 26th, 2013

Each minute, each hour, each day that passes brings me closer to seeing Marilyn Manson live. There is however, a bonus as well. One I dare not share, lest my poison infects another victim. In both cases, "closer" is the operative word, one I long for, one I wish could be simpler.

Staying away from drugs seems to be a losing battle. While I have cut down considerably, the cravings are only getting stronger. I also have yet to find a concrete reason to quit. "It's bad for you" is a bullshit reason. So is salt, fatty foods, alcohol, cigarettes, too much sun, and too little sun. Drugs are bad for those that do not respect the power of them. Those that go far beyond their limit and hurt themselves. Yes, I believe there is a responsible way of using drugs, and I also believe it follows that there is such thing as a *functional addict*. Some of the most famous people used drugs. Sigmund Freud, for one, praised cocaine. He also was a sexual deviant, but that is beside the point.

- XV

Who Saw This One Coming?
January 28th, 2013

I wish there was a sarcasm font. Once again I have relapsed. Details are irrelevant. I am weak, and I will be for a while. I am trying to become better, to rebuild my mind. I have started writing a book, where it will take me I do not know, but at least it is exercising my mind. I'm also signed up for a psychology course starting on the 1st of February. I'm hoping to regain some of my mental faculties.

Marilyn Manson is tomorrow. The anticipation is killing me, in a good way. I have heard every single one of his songs at least a hundred times and seeing him live will be the culmination of almost a decade of my fandom. I will post a show review after, but a special thanks to the wonderful and talented and selfless (*name withheld*) for, well, everything!

- XV

My Life Is Complete
January 31st, 2013

The concert was everything I expected and more. It was perhaps the best night of my life, and I got to share it with a great friend (you know who you are). I was nearly in tears as the Intro music for Manson's set began. It didn't feel real until I saw his silhouette on the black curtain hiding the stage. As they broke into "Hey Cruel World" the curtain dropped, and for the first time ever, after almost a decade of obsession, I saw Manson in the flesh. From our seats we had a good vantage point of the stage, although Twiggy seemed to like hiding behind the light tower to the right of the stage. Even at the age of 44, after 24 years of playing show after show, releasing 8 records (plus bonus material and EPs), and suffering at the hands of the media and girlfriends, he did not disappoint. He emerged wearing a black mask and began to scream the lyrics. The live show sound was perfect, especially for such a small venue. His props and costume changes were incredible, as was his stage presence. He has not lost the ultra-sexual "groove", proven by both a brief period of humping the speakers as well as putting his hand down his pants as the crowd cheered.

Sharing this with a good friend was the cherry on top. I knew I would make a fan out of her, and seeing her enjoy Marilyn Manson (almost) as much as I do was a great feeling. We got several pictures and about 30 minutes of video to remember this amazing experience by. (I am working on getting the video on Youtube at this very moment). That night was not about the grueling traffic, sketchy weather conditions, or the money. It was about seeing the Antichrist Superstar himself. It was about the experience, the laughs, the rock, the shock, and most of all the memories. I doubt I will ever be able to repay my dear friend for what she did that night, but I at least hope she sees exactly what seeing Manson meant to me. After years of having his music to fall back on, I finally saw him in a glorious orgy of make-up, music, playmates, drugs, and everything else that made that night, January 29th, 2013, perhaps the best night of my life. When suffering from unrelenting depression and pain, even the smallest things can make a world of difference. This was monumental. This was my dream. This was worth every second, every bit of pain.

Thank you, B

- XV

Hypocrisy - An Amusing Look at the Mainstream Television Paradox
January 31st, 2013

Hypocrisy is an interesting thing. People say one thing, then do something to go against it. It's like an alcoholic that tells people drinking is bad.

Television is the most amusing example of this "phenomenon". I watched an episode of Criminal Minds and was baffled by the censorship, as well as the lack there-of. They showed brutal, bloody crime scenes with decapitated corpses and bloody knives, but later on censored the word "bitch". A big WTF??? to the network for that. Further, commercials for beer cannot show someone actually drinking the beer, but in trailers for upcoming movies can show violent explosions, gunfire, and other suggestive content. The shows that have a "Parental Discretion Advised" warning before it are really telling people that the network's idea of what is offensive may be in there, but does not warn about other blatantly "mature" content.

This is an amusing statement about our society, its relaxed views of violence, and the random censorship of certain TV content. So let me summarize: bloody, headless corpses are okay, but the word "ass" or "bitch" needs to be censored. One network can show graphic content without a "Parental Advisory", while another needs to cover their asses (excuse the coarse language). How are these standards decided? Who decides what is okay for people to see and hear? Want pure, real, uncensored violence? Turn on the news. The news is perhaps the most graphic thing on television. Stories of murder, rape, terrorism, and chaos are covered, while other stories containing less violence are slapped in at the end, a mere footnote.

TV, you amuse me.

- XV

The Inevitable Fall
February 1st, 2013

Sometimes, now more than ever, I feel like a ghost masquerading as a human being. Playing out some fantasy of clinging to life, going through the motions, trying to fool people into thinking it is alive. This play is getting towards the end, when the curtains close and the ghost is thrown back into non-existence. The ghost knew all along that it was no longer alive. It thought it could play along and that the show would never end. It was wrong.

The ghost should have seen that it can only act for so long until people catch on. It's not just those once close to the ghost that get caught in the explosion, it's everyone who comes into contact with it. The explosion has just gone off. It's done. It is once again time to slip back into nothingness and let the world move on, unharmed by the ghost's destruction.

Fuck it. The crowd all saw it coming anyways.

- XV

Time to Enter the Surreal
February 2nd, 2013

I can't handle what I did, what I've done.
It's all catching up to me now.
Time to drink the nectar of disassociation.
And leave this place behind....
For a while.

- XV

Success
February 4th, 2013

It worked!

for a while. Where did my weekend go?

Rinse and repeat.

- XV

From The Ashes
February 6th, 2013

It's time to make a big-boy decision. Do I let this pain win, or do I step up and beat it? Every time I get a little bit of motivation to get better, it is usually stomped back down by harsh reality. If a time will ever come where I can beat this, I may never know. Maybe I don't want to. Maybe this is who I am meant to be. Some kind of martyr. If it is what I am meant to be, then I will go down in flames. Set this fucking world on fire. Otherwise I guess I have to find a way to beat this. It's clear what the easy choice is. Maybe I will stick with that until I can see more clearly, or am given a reason to fight for something more.

- XV

Ties That Bind
February 8th, 2013

What is it that keeps the past so close to me? People and things long gone still affect me more than I'd like to say. Sure, the past has a place in who you are presently, and by extension, in the future, but where do I draw the line? The people, they are gone, moved on. Or have they? That nagging question keeps me stuck in those days. I had my chance.

- XV

A Return to Honesty, As I Intended from the Start
February 10th, 2013

I seemed to have waivered from my initial path of blunt, brutal honesty. While every word I write is the truth, I seem to be hiding a lot of truth. I have swept it under the rug and censored my posts, avoiding the pain and reality associated with the truth. On the outside I am maintaining the same facade, for other people's benefit. Sometimes I slip up and drop the mask, allowing people to see the true ugliness underneath. I do not mean ugly in the "not beautiful" sense, I mean it in the violent, angry, and grotesque way. I have fallen too far, covered up too much, and caused too much pain to tell you that I am okay. That would be a monumental lie. I am tired of lying. The pain is relentless in its severity and scope. The fact that I have made it so far even amazes me. I have seen everyone I know run away, hiding from the monster they see in me. That's okay. Fuck them. Less people I have to continue this masquerade around.

What specifically is making me this way is unclear. Perhaps it is an amalgamation of every knife stabbed into my back, slowly twisting. Maybe there is no reason. Maybe it is just the way I am. Regardless, I will admit now I am not okay. It will not be okay. This is just the start. Hold on for dear life. Or let go, as they all do. Makes no difference in the end.

I have pulled the hammer back, who will pull the trigger first? You, or I?

- XV

Freud Was Right
February 10th, 2013

Someone asked me today what I was afraid of. Snakes? Spiders? Heights? I was hard pressed to find something that I was afraid of. The answer, however, is quite obvious. I am afraid of myself. Mostly afraid of what has been tucked away deep in my subconscious, but also of what would happen if it were to spill into my conscious mind. There is so much I have repressed. Feelings, memories, thoughts... Can I continue to hold these back? or are the floodgates about to burst? It would surely end in catastrophe. I am afraid of what I have the potential to do, I am afraid of those nightmares that can easily become reality, I am afraid of losing what control I have over myself and my actions.

- XV

Happy Birthday
February 12th, 2013

A very happy birthday to a close friend!! I hope you have a good one, and many more to come :)

Much love,

- XV

Existing
February 13th, 2013

I feel, for the most part, that I am only just existing. I am part of a continuum but no more, potentially less. As I have said before, I play my part in this masquerade, keeping a smile on my face and the demons down. To be honest, I am growing tired of this masquerade. I no longer want to play the role of a martyr - mentally sick and socially alienated. I go through life doing what needs to be done to fulfill my role in society. The bare minimum for someone to be alive. I do not wish for bigger and better things anymore, and I do not pretend to look forward to a bright future. I feel mechanical; a robot programmed to get by. But enough of that. Blah blah blah.

However, I cannot help but wonder... what if? Hmmm... Is it even worth pursuing, knowing who I really am? Knowing my self-destructive ways, and of course all of the collateral damage caused by the chaos I create.

I cannot even form a thought right now. Maybe my next post will shed more light on what I am trying to say. All I know is that I am tired of feeling this way, tired of the pain, and tired of being alone. Pshhhht. *weep*

- XV

Gun Me Down
February 14th, 2013

It is not paranoia if they are actually out to get you. This particular post is for someone who used to be everything to me. Close friends for over 12 years, yet it seemed easy when you gunned me down and threw my corpse in the trash. I cannot completely blame you, however. I did a lot of wrong during that time. Difference is, I accept it. You run. Like a pedophile chasing a school bus you run. Like a cockroach you hide. You move from place to place, person to person until it gets to be too much, then you run some more. It would seem (to the untrained eye) that you have finally settled down. Congrats... Knocked up?

Anyway, your hypocrisy has always amused me. The perfect Christian, except for those lines of coke you came to enjoy so much. And the sex, the violence, as well as the general debauchery that defined our time together. Then suddenly it was no longer good. So you ran. As usual. Now, you are hiding. You can cut me from your life, but there will always be traces of me in your veins.

- XV

Happy Valentine's Day
February 14th, 2013

It amazes me how shameless corporations are. They come up with this 'holiday', telling you to be romantic, love your partner, and spoil them. It is just like Christmas and Easter... It is all about consumerism. If you really need one day out of the year to be romantic, then maybe you should not be together. Just saying.

Then you have your singles that see this day as their loneliness being thrown in their faces. Suck it up, dickweed. It is just a day on the calendar. It is a day created to make people spend money, as if material goods can measure the 'love' and 'romance' between two people.

Oh, and to add onto my last post, your birthday is tomorrow. I hope it is a horrible day.

- XV

<u>Suppression</u>
February 15th, 2013

Lately, a theme has been emerging in my posts. This theme is "the past". Looking at it on a large scale, I have come to realize that there is blackness where memories should be. It's like playing a film but most of the scenes have been cut out. This not only interests me, but confounds me as well. Have I subconsciously supressed those memories that hurt? I know something happened, but the details seem to elude me. My brain has been a victim of an on-going psychological blitzkrieg. It has been hammered by drugs, pain, and horrible memories for years now. Trying to sort it out is like trying to untangle a rope that is a thousand miles long. Bits and pieces come forth, but whole parts of my life seem to have disappeared, leaving me unable to account for that time. Sure, I have my journals.

But they are only a guide, the details have escaped me. It is frustrating to try to remember what happened and why. It would shed some light onto why I feel the way I feel, and why I am the way I am. Perhaps my brain has blocked those puzzle pieces, and maybe for my protection. All I know is that I have lived lives I do not remember. People have come and gone from my life and I do not remember why. Cataclysms leaving burning, gaping wounds that will never heal. My amnesia, whatever the cause, seems to leave me hemorrhaging memories and truths.

I feel exsanguinated, empty.

If I cannot fill my past, how the hell do I fill the future? I have entered relationships and left a burning pile of scraps every time. I seem destined to be alone, alienated because of who I am. The past is supposed to make me who I am now. If that is true.... then maybe there is a reason I have supressed it.

Help.

Please.

- XV

Neglect
February 19th, 2013

Although I have managed to keep this journal going, I have neglected to keep my personal, written journal up to date. When I open it and go to write, my mind empties. Words escape me and I feel fear. I am afraid to write in there, after over 3 years of writing, I struggle to write a single sentence. This fear is irrational, phantom, but tangible. I do not know what it is I am afraid of. I have literally put my blood into these journals, written down my darkest secrets and deepest fears. This neglect may be my way of escaping that, but I just do not know. Do I really think those words I write will matter?
Will someday make some kind of difference? I highly doubt they will. They are just my words etched onto paper, a way to clear my head. Now it feels like a burden.

- XV

Down, Down
February 19th, 2013

I feel like something terrible is about to happen. What is left of my heart is stuck in my throat. It seems inevitable. I don't know what. I don't know when. But it will happen. Maybe I will finally burn this fucking world to the ground.

- XV

Devour
February 20th, 2013

"I'll swallow up all of you
like a big bottle of big, big pills
but, you're the one that I should never take
but I can't sleep until I devour you
I can't sleep until I devour you."

- Devour, Marilyn Manson

If history has taught me anything, it is that where there is desire, there is weakness. Where there is love, there is pain. Where there is me, there is chaos. I can liken my past relationships to a brutal addiction. Chasing the high until there is nothing left but destruction. Then the next craving comes and the cycle repeats. Even when I know I should stay clear of someone, something takes over and I ignore my better judgement. I don't believe after all the pain and heartbreak that I am capable of love. What I do feel seems synthetic. It always leaves me wanting more, but I know the consequences of succumbing to the desire. Maybe I am supposed to be alone, I have just been too stubborn to see it. Maybe she is just better off without me. Maybe they all are.

- XV

Give Me a Reason
February 20th, 2013

Shockingly, I have been clean for a few weeks. Sure, lack of money is a factor, but the cravings haven't been as powerful as usual. I still experience insane anxiety that has me reaching for the Xanax, however. I look to the future and see grey. There are no certainties. I have no plans, no goals, just fears. The past is a good tool for predicting the future, and it looks like I am screwed. Don't call me a pessimist, just a realist. Balance has never been a part of my life. If one part is going well, all other parts tend to be fucked up. What reason could I have for "getting better". That is, bowing to social pressures and quitting drugs, going to school, and being a good little citizen. Whether it is because of my borderline personality disorder or not, I have come to accept and even embrace the chaos that follows me around. Give me a reason to change. There are few people who can, but I could never ask that of them. Especially knowing my history, how damaging I am.

"And I was a hand grenade that never stopped exploding."
- Mechanical Animals, Marilyn Manson

Pretty much. So anyway, inevitably I will soon get my cheque and likely be faced with the age-old question: *To use, or not to use.* I know what I "should" do, but that seems to differ greatly from what I want to do, and what I actually do in the end. So give me a reason to say no. Clearly drugs have had a detrimental effect on my life, but so have other things. I am my own greatest enemy, and it is not the drugs I fear, but what hides deep in my subconscious, and even more so what escapes my subconscious. Even when I had 'love', that is someone who was around and cared about me (for whatever reason), for the most part I still used. It's not like some girl will enter my life and clean me up. History shows that I will most likely cut them up with my broken self. I feel alone, but I know better than to pursue a relationship. It's not someone else's burden to 'fix' me. If that is even a possibility, of course. I am content (not happy, but content) being alone if it means one less shattered heart. My own poisonous nature is my cross to bear, and always will be. Of course there is the loophole that I could find someone already as damaged as I am, but I'd be more likely to capture Bigfoot with a roll of dental floss. Let me put it mathematically (as my obnoxious way of being dryly sarcastic):

(damaged) x (not damaged) = destruction
(damaged) x (damaged) = damaged²

Therefore,

me = fucked

Do the math, it works

- XV

Indifference
February 21st, 2013

I can pretend to care, I can also pretend not to. But when it comes down to it, I know who I am on the inside, for the most part. This was inevitable, as it always will be. Why fight? I don't really give a fuck.

- XV

Once In A While, I Am Shocked...
February 22nd, 2013

I recently reunited with an old friend with whom I had lost touch. As days go by, I lose faith in people, in myself, in relationships, friendships, and pretty much everything else. It was very refreshing to be remembered that amongst the smoking wreckage I call a past, that there may be one, maybe even more people that haven't completely given up on me. I realize I am an expert at isolation and shutting people out, but last night I was reminded (for the first time in a long time) what it is like to have a good friend, accepting and understanding.

Of all the ridiculous surprises that pop up in my life, this was one that I can call a good surprise.

- XV

Leave a Scar
February 26th, 2013

"It's not like I made myself a list
of new and different ways to murder your heart.
I'm just a painting that's still wet,
if you touch me I'll be smeared, you'll be stained,
stained for the rest of your life."

As poisonous as I feel, sometimes a little bit of light seeps through the shroud. It's rare, but it happens. A friend recently wrote an amazing poem (word on the street is that it was inspired by me) and that was perhaps the best gift I have ever received. Not only did I love the very Manson-esque word play, but she made me realize a lot about myself. I often get too much into my own head, I have never really had someone on the outside looking in put it in their own words. Even now I am having writer's block trying to make this post. I know what I want to say, but the words are playing a twisted game of hide and seek.

I think the lyrics above say what I am trying to say, in general. I seem to leave a lot of lives stained, I don't know if I will ever be "dry" enough to be with someone and not destroy them.

- XV

Enough
February 28th, 2013

I have had enough of being weak. Enough of the dreams that chain me to the past. Memories turning into nightmares, reminding me of all that I have lost. I am growing more fearful of sleep. It is when my subconscious takes over and has free reign over me. It is a trickster, a thought demon that plagues me with things better left behind. But the past seems to never be the past, completely. There is too much pain, too much chaos, too much that haunts my dreams to be able to move on and let go. I would give anything to forget, to move on, to be able to stomp out the embers of my past. But what else can I do? It is as much a part of me as the present. It has shaped me into this mess that I am. Now I truly believe in curses. They attack every part of my being, and I am left broken and weak. Please move on. Please let go.

- XV

Things Better Left Buried
March 1st, 2013

There is a feeling I have, one with potentially horrible consequences. Is it something better left buried deep inside, or is it something worth trying? I know she is worth it, but once again I quote my history of destruction as good reason to try to let this go. But a big part of me does not want to. It is an impossible decision, even more impossible to predict the outcome. Maybe I am reading too much into certain things, certain words, and certain actions. There is so much of me that knows this is better left alone, but there will always be a part of me that wonders what if? Decisions, decisions.

- XV

Evidence
March 2nd, 2013

"You have eyes that lead me on
And a body that shows me death
Your lips look like they were made
For something else but
They just suck my breath
I want your pain
To taste why you're ashamed
And I know you're not just what you say to me
And I'm not the only moment you're made of
You're so sudden and sweet
All legs, knuckle, knees
Head's blown clean off
Your mouth's paid off
Fuck me 'til we know it's unsafe
And we'll paint
Over the evidence
I want you wanting me
I want what I see in your eyes
So give me something to be scared of
Don't give me something to satisfy"

- Evidence, Marilyn Manson

Today I Am Dirty
March 2nd, 2013

The Nobodies has always been the quintessential anthem for alienated youth. At least, it was for me since first hearing it before I was even in high school. The lyrics are simple and short, but encompass all of the feelings often felt by (for lack of a better term) 'people like me'. I cannot remember a time when I felt like somebody, like I knew who I was. Feeling like dirt is just par for the course. I find it interesting, however, that there seems to be two different interpretations of the song's chorus. The first:

*"Fear the Nobodies, wanna be somebodies,
when we're dead, they'll know just who we are."*

as well as:

*"We're the Nobodies, wanna be somebodies
we're dead, we know just who we are."*

A careful listen to the song shows the second chorus to be the one Manson belts out. The first chorus also sounds good, and fits with the theme of the song, but perfectly displays people's ignorance to Manson's message.

The entire album 'Holywood' is undoubtedly a mockery of religion and the mainstream media, with self-defeating undertones. Once again, ignorance takes a ride when people listen to the lyrics of this album and take it literally.

*"This was never my world, you took the angel away,
I'd kill myself to make everybody pay."*

It's symbolism... metaphors. A statement that is all too true. When you do something horrific, and the cameras are watching, and in the end you off yourself, you become a celebrity. Despite this, I still feel connected to the lyrics in this album. However, I do to each album, but each in a different way.

Anyway, just something to think about the next time you see someone at their lowest. Maybe *'nothing's gonna change the world'*, but Manson (in his own way) tells you that you do not have to face it alone. That feeling that way, however unpleasant, is not wrong or weak, but just a part of the human condition. I can say with honesty that without Marilyn Manson, and his lyrical brilliance, I would have been dead long ago.

- XV

<u>"Friendship"</u>
March 3rd, 2013

I define friendship as giving someone a knife and expecting them not to stab it deep into your back. Most friendships are frail, for that very reason. All these people that called me 'friend' have each thrust the knife into my back and walked away. I take credit for my part in it. I let my guard down, and expected too much. Although, expecting a good friend to stick around when things get hard is not too much to ask, in my books. I have systematically lost most of my 'friends'. When things in my life got hard, they stabbed and ran, leaving me alone to suffer my fate. I feel that I am better off anyways, the less friends you have, the less chance of being fucked over. This is not pessimism, although it does look like it. It is just a fact of life. Some friends are leeches, and will use you for whatever purpose until you can no longer fulfill their needs. Others are the ones you would call a best friend but turns out they are only looking out for themselves. In the end, all people do.

I used to torture myself, call myself a failure for losing so many people. But looking back, not only am I better off in the end, the way I am, so are they. The moment I dropped my mask and said "Here I am." was the moment these 'friends' of mine started running. Again I go back to my role in all of this. With so many chaotic relationships, so much drama, so many drugs... I am better off alone. But one good friend has proven me wrong and has stuck by me (after a long period of non-communication). She still is there for me, and I am not afraid of the metaphorical knife I have given her, because I know it will remain holstered. There are very few people I trust, but she is one of the few.

Maybe I am just bitter because of my past, because of losing so many people I was once close to. From time to time, when my mind wanders, I can still feel the sting and the empty void left by people I thought were friends. Or maybe I am just trying to justify being a loner. Who knows?

- XV

Hitting the Wall
March 3rd, 2013

I feel like I have hit a wall. My depression feels more pronounced, my fatigue is crippling, and the emptiness is overwhelming. I have gone through several phases like this, but each time it seems harder to get back up. My routine is mind-numbingly boring and always the same. People always have all kinds of advice like 'get out of the house'. I can barely get out of bed. Easier said than done. I have not used drugs for quite some time (feels like forever anyways). I feel without them I am back to my lowest. The drugs offered an escape, they offered freedom from the barbed-wire cage of depression. Without them, I feel weaker, as messed up as that would sound to most people. It is not messed up to me, though. There is a reason I used.

Now I sit in the wreckage, trapped, nowhere to go, nothing to do to fix this. I see no exit, no future, nothing. I will not lie to myself anymore about that. Going through the motions, pretending that I am living is finally catching up to me. It is like a thick blanket of fog has rolled in, and I am trapped in the middle. That is my truth.

- XV

Demon Eyes
March 4th, 2013

I had a dream last night, one that I am sure I will never forget. The first thing I remember is standing in a bathroom, everything was white and it was hard to see. I was looking at my hands, covered in blood. I had to wipe blood off the mirror to see myself. Looking back at me was a grotesque version of myself. My skin was pale and covered in blood. I could not tell if it was mine or not. My eyes were pure black, demon eyes, and sunken back into my skull. A large pentagram was carved into my chest but was not bleeding. I walked out of the bathroom into this giant room that reminded me of an empty airplane hangar. I looked and saw dozens of piles of bodies, butchered beyond recognition. There must have been hundreds. The bloody knife I realized I was suddenly holding felt heavy as I walked around the piles of corpses, zig-zagging amongst the pools of blood and ripped flesh. I was not afraid of the scene. Maggots were crawling in and out of the gaping cuts made in the bodies. When I got across the massive room, a wall of mirrors stood in front of me. I was pale, thin, frail, and bloody. The demon eyes pierced into me. I knew I had done this, but was I possessed? I dropped the knife and fell to my knees. Suddenly a column of black smoke came shooting out of my mouth and I collapsed.

Needless to say, I woke up shaking with a cold sweat. It all seemed so real, and those piercing demon eyes are imprinted on my mind. I ran to the bathroom and my eyes were blue again, with the usual sunken darkness around them from my insomnia. I am not one to believe in dream analysis, but holy shit. Maybe I need to see a professional, or at least cut down on the horror movies.

- XV

So Far...
March 4th, 2013

So far I have revealed things about me that nobody else knows. Things about me that I have kept secret for a long time. Things about me that scare even myself. What is the point of it all? I do not know, exactly, but I feel it will all culminate into some sort of story that will give you an understanding of what is going on in my head. Most people would read this and be repulsed. The truth often is repulsing. I must admit that I have left out details, for my protection and for those who may read this. If the details were relevant, I would have had a harder time keeping them out. But the constant chatter filling my head is impossible to contain. If I were to tell you half of the things that go through my head, you would likely pack up and run, run as the others have in my life. But you stay, and that has stifled some of the thoughts, but I will never be free of them.

My mind is my worst enemy, and if anyone is actually following my posts, they would see a scattered mess of a deranged mind. Hidden in consonants and vowels, buried deep in metaphor and verse. Perhaps a cry for help has been muffled by self-censorship. I am used to being the fuck up, the bad guy, the martyr. It has been so long I have forgotten who I used to be. The person that once was happy, social, and in university is long gone, replaced by an entity. A shadow of my former self, beaten down and mutilated by the events of the past four years. I no longer feel human, I feel like a ghost. Too stubborn to admit he is dead and only going through the motions of life. Read these words and see that I am not just a danger to myself.

Reparation seems like an impossible dream. Shrouded in this dystopia I have forgotten true happiness, and what it feels like to love and be loved. Circumstance has made the chances of that happening impossible. So what do I do? I am not happy. But I am not suicidal. I will only just continue to punish myself by 'living' the same life, day after day. Counting down, and down, and down... Until something finally happens. I want to think that there is hope on the horizon, but the fog is too dense to see ahead.

- XV

<u>**Une Annonce**</u>
March 4th, 2013

It is time I accepted my place in the world. There are no complaints here, no self-pity, only truths. Uncensored truths. People say I have potential, but potential is nothing without will, the drive to be better, and most of all, hope. So begins a new chapter in my life. No more fighting the inevitable, I do not have the strength. No more wearing the masks for other people's benefit. All the masks do is distort who I really am. No more pretending everything is okay. I am empty and tired. There is a massive hole where my heart once was, sounds of a heart that once beat barely echo throughout my damaged body. The scars are a testament to my pain, both psychological and physical. I have tried for years to balance my life, to find happiness. Every time I think I have found it, it explodes in front of me. I cannot deny my role in the chaos, nor can they. I am tired. Tired of the depression, the therapy, the pills, the stigma, the insomnia, the anxiety... I am tired of people telling me what is best for me, tired of trying to meet their expectations, and tired of hiding who I really am. I am sick... mostly psychologically, but it is seeping into physicality.

All that these past few years have brought me is chaos. Blood-soaked sheets, scars that will never heal, loss of will, loss of faith, loss of people I thought had my back. I am afraid to trust anybody anymore. And they should be afraid too. Look at what I have done. Look at the path of destruction behind me. And why? For what? For nothing. It is all senseless, meaningless, and pointless. It has left me in shambles, and trust me when I say that all the king's horses and men cannot put me back together again. Each failed relationship took a piece from me, and now I am like a jigsaw puzzle missing a few pieces needed to complete it. It is clear that I am meant to be the loner I am. It is safer for everyone. Maybe one day I will learn to live as what I have become, but for now, the prognosis is not good.

Sure, the drugs can be to blame. They have been the best and worst thing in this sad story. After the escape comes the crash and the fall, and you find yourself back at square one. To be honest, at this point I would rather live a short life in the bliss of the high than a long life spent miserable and in pain. Call me selfish, I call you ignorant.

This is my truth, my confession of sorts. Nothing censored, no desperate attempts for pity, no desire for sympathy... Just cold, hard fact. Think I am wrong? Think I have not told the whole truth? Prove it.

- XV

Repercussions and a Nightmare
March 5th, 2013

I do not know what to think. My last post was honest, but still did not convey exactly how I am feeling. I appreciate a certain friend's optimism, but it is realism that counts, at least to me. Now this friend knows how I feel, to some extent, and it will not change anything. I do not expect it to.

I had another dream last night that most would call a nightmare. I call it a normal dream, for me at least. Once again it started with me in a blank white bathroom staring into the mirror, pure black demon eyes stared back at me. I was pale, expressionless. After a while I smiled and lifted up my arm, realizing there was a large butcher knife in my hand. My blank stare turned into a smile as I put the knife to my throat and slowly made a deep cut from left to right. The blood that poured out was thick and black. I continued to smile, with no control over my body. It seemed like forever before my smile disappeared and I choked out "How do you like me now?" Everything went black and once again I woke up in a cold sweat, shaking and feeling my throat to make sure it was still intact.

Again, I will not analyze that dream. I can admit I am afraid to. My subconscious is crawling with horrors I can only imagine. Those are better kept locked up.

- XV

I Have To Look Up Just To See Hell
March 5th, 2013

*"You can take me,
The grave can take me
The earth is waiting to eat us alive
I love you damaged,
I need human wreckage
I have to look up
Just to see Hell"*

- I Have To Look Up Just To See Hell, Marilyn Manson

From my vantage point all I see is black. Looking forward I see nothing. Maybe because a future does not exist. I know you will not like the words I say here, optimism is one of your good qualities. The fact is I feel like I will never escape this endless cycle. Day after day, the same old shit. I am going nowhere, and to be honest, all drive that I once had to be something has long since gone. Still, I put on my mask and pretend everything is okay. But recently I have decided to rid of the masks, rid of the lies I tell myself to get me through.

I would be content living in a world of drugs, constantly numb.... I am tired of feeling. Pain, emptiness, sadness, blah blah. Unfortunately that is not a possibility for me. I must try to endure, but even that is getting harder and harder to do every day that passes.

Relationships? Blah. I will only destroy them. But at the same time I feel it is what I need. It is some pathetic need for human interaction, and attention. To be honest, I do not think I can move forward with a relationship when the past is pulling me down... still. Their names flood my head, poisoning my thoughts, bringing up horrid memories I have fought to forget.

This is torture.

- XV

You Can Try, but You Won't
March 5th, 2013

We try to pry life from Death
We try to pretend a ghost is a man
We try to sweep it all under the rug
We wear the mask, to please them all
We take the high road
We take a high of our own
We try to fix what cannot be fixed
We look in vain for answers
We take pain in stride
We let it destroy our lives
We will not admit we were wrong
We will not admit we are wrong
Love is like a ticking time-bomb
Love is like a razor blade
Love is everything
Love is nothing
Your heart is so cold, I can see my breath
Your heart is so cold, I can see my breath

You are the Great Destroyer
Your heart is so cold I can see my breath
We lie to each other
We lie to ourselves
Life is but a cruel game
Life is but a cruel game
Life is short
Life is too long, for some
Death is the end
Death is the enigma
Death is yes and no
Death is the great release
The future is blurry
The future is unknown
The future is known
The future means nothing
We are all fucked
We all fuck, fuck, fuck

We all fuck over
We are all fucked

- XV

Tourniquet
March 6th, 2013

"Take your hatred out on me
Make your victim my head
You never ever believed in me
I am your tourniquet."

- Tourniquet, Marilyn Manson

A tourniquet is only a temporary fix. It stops the bleeding, for a while.

Every day I feel psychological pain, like a gaping wound in my soul that no tourniquet can slow the bleeding. Every part of me is broken, many parts beyond repair. Over three years ago I let someone use me as their punching bag. I took all the hits, and she just kept throwing punches. I would let her take her issues out on me, I did not mind. I thought I was in love. Love makes you fucking stupid. You cannot see the negative things about the person you love, you can only see what you want to see - the good things. In the end, I found myself fighting to find something good about her to hold on to, but with one final punch, it was gone. I was down. Over three years later I have yet to get back up. Self-abuse and my chaotic relationships have been constantly pushing me back down. It has weakened me, destroyed much of me, but somehow I am still here.

Looking back, I am still unsure if it was worth all this pain. Everything I was years ago is gone. It has been replaced by grotesque, mangled parts, reassembled into something horrific. Beware.

- XV

Speechless
March 7th, 2013

I say nothing because I know it will not make a difference. I keep quiet because I have screwed up enough already. I am speechless because of you.

- XV

I Am Among No One
March 8th, 2013

... No one.

Part choice, part circumstance, part whatever. If I had a nickel for every day spent sitting in this room staring at this screen, I would be a fucking millionaire. Frankly, I am shocked when I go outside and don't burst into flames. There is still hope for that I guess. I do not ask for pity, or a strained "Awe". I look for a way out of this, a way to end the cycle. So far, there are not very many options, and the ones that do exist are not preferable.

- XV

No Reflection
March 8th, 2013

When I look in the mirror, I am starting to see what I used to hide deep inside myself coming to the surface. Eyes dark and sunken, skin pale, stare blank. I feel like I am turning into a corpse. The damage I have done to my body is showing, and the stress I am feeling now more than ever is eating away at me. For the first time in a long time I crave nothing. No drugs, no booze, no cigarettes; not even food or sleep. I do not know what I am becoming, but I feel like eventually there will be no reflection staring back at me. Maybe just the silhouette of who I once was. I have only ideas of what would pour life back into me, but it all seems uncertain. I guess I am used to uncertainty, used to being in this place, but for some reason, the effect on my body and mind has increased exponentially.

I don't know which me that I love. Got no reflection.

"Show myself how to make a noose
A gun's cliché, and a razor too
I'm not a deathshare vacation, vacant station
Made of scars and filled with my old wounds"

- No Reflection, Marilyn Manson

- XV

Fucking Finances
March 9th, 2013

I have no reservations about declaring that **'money is the new fascism'**. It takes over every part of your life and sucks you fucking dry. It throws you into a pit that you are forced to dig deeper and deeper until you realize that it is impossible to get out.

Find a job? I would have an easier time finding fucking Bigfoot in my fridge. Fucking downright depressed right now. I don't know what to do. I wish I could live in isolation, no taxes, no bullshit. Live off the land. Then again I would not last a week.
Fucking finances.

- XV

Deja Vu
March 9th, 2013

I am wasting away here. It is getting worse every day. All these years and nothing to show for it but a bunch of scars and a psychiatric diagnosis. I have been beaten down and now I have no desire to get back up. Maybe I am getting repetitive in my posts, but not much happens that is noteworthy. I wish there was. Someone to write about, or something.

As hard as this may be to believe, my life was better on drugs. The cocaine gave me energy, euphoria... The MDMA gave me synthetic happiness, which is better than real pain. They gave me a chance to escape this existence for a while at least, and now that I am no longer using, I feel pushed down and exhausted. I cannot afford to start using again, however. I cannot even afford a pack of cigarettes. This is a place I never thought I would be. I want out. By any means necessary.

- XV

every day spent sitting in this room staring at this screen, I would be a fucking millionaire. Frankly, I am shocked when I go outside and don't burst into flames. There is still hope for that I guess. I do not ask for pity, or a strained "Awe". I look for a way out of this, a way to end the cycle. So far, there are not very many options, and the ones that do exist are not preferable.

- XV

No Reflection
March 8th, 2013

When I look in the mirror, I am starting to see what I used to hide deep inside myself coming to the surface. Eyes dark and sunken, skin pale, stare blank. I feel like I am turning into a corpse. The damage I have done to my body is showing, and the stress I am feeling now more than ever is eating away at me. For the first time in a long time I crave nothing. No drugs, no booze, no cigarettes; not even food or sleep. I do not know what I am becoming, but I feel like eventually there will be no reflection staring back at me. Maybe just the silhouette of who I once was. I have only ideas of what would pour life back into me, but it all seems uncertain. I guess I am used to uncertainty, used to being in this place, but for some reason, the effect on my body and mind has increased exponentially.

I don't know which me that I love. Got no reflection.

"Show myself how to make a noose
A gun's cliché, and a razor too
I'm not a deathshare vacation, vacant station
Made of scars and filled with my old wounds"

- No Reflection, Marilyn Manson

- XV

Fucking Finances
March 9th, 2013

I have no reservations about declaring that **'money is the new fascism'**. It takes over every part of your life and sucks you fucking dry. It throws you into a pit that you are forced to dig deeper and deeper until you realize that it is impossible to get out.

Find a job? I would have an easier time finding fucking Bigfoot in my fridge. Fucking downright depressed right now. I don't know what to do. I wish I could live in isolation, no taxes, no bullshit. Live off the land. Then again I would not last a week.
Fucking finances.

- XV

Deja Vu
March 9th, 2013

I am wasting away here. It is getting worse every day. All these years and nothing to show for it but a bunch of scars and a psychiatric diagnosis. I have been beaten down and now I have no desire to get back up. Maybe I am getting repetitive in my posts, but not much happens that is noteworthy. I wish there was. Someone to write about, or something.

As hard as this may be to believe, my life was better on drugs. The cocaine gave me energy, euphoria... The MDMA gave me synthetic happiness, which is better than real pain. They gave me a chance to escape this existence for a while at least, and now that I am no longer using, I feel pushed down and exhausted. I cannot afford to start using again, however. I cannot even afford a pack of cigarettes. This is a place I never thought I would be. I want out. By any means necessary.

- XV

Fantastic Planet
March 10th, 2013

Last night brought a nice surprise in the form of a certain powdery substance. Afterwards we popped some Xanax and smoked some weed, then laid down and let the high hit. I put on the Fantastic Planet soundtrack, which is trippy as shit, and turned on my LED Jellyfish Lamp. I have never been so relaxed (despite the slight tachycardia from the blow). It was the vacation I mentioned before that I needed.
Plus I found a Nintendo 64 Emulator for the computer, so I can rock Goldeneye once again. I can see few better ways of spending my time.

- XV

Exsanguination
March 11th, 2013

'I chased after them. I could easily have caught them, but I liked the idea of toying with them first. Like a lion chasing a gazelle, I waited until the weakest fell behind and took her out. My mouth latched onto her throat and I pulled the blood from her body. I still was not satisfied, so I continued the chase. I caught back up in a matter of seconds and leapt in front of the three remaining 'people'. I was soaked in blood and smiling at them, deciding who to devour next. The guy made the choice for me as he was the first to try to run away. Him I would just break and kill, male blood was too sour anyways. Two down, two to go. I was still thirsty for more. One was a heavy brunette who was not very attractive. I could smell her blood... too many calories for my taste. I snapped her neck and she dropped to the ground. I turned to the remaining girl. The reason I was here. I saved her for last, like a dessert. I walked towards her as she cowered in terror. She was at least smart enough to not try to run, so she stood there, the fear tangible in her gaze. I could smell her blood, it was intoxicating. I licked the blood from my lips and grabbed her by the arm. She only stared as I sank my teeth into her pale skin. No blood had ever been this good, this piquant. I drained every last bit of blood from her limp body and she dropped to the ground. Her eyes were still wide open in terror even though there was no life left in her.'

And that is when I woke up. What is it with my dreams lately? My medications cause lucid dreaming, but recently it has been, well, disturbing (as you can tell). But there is a bit on intrigue there.

- XV

This World = Facepalm
March 11th, 2013

I watch the news sometimes, I see people go about their lives, I watch horrible commercials and the only thing I can do is shake my head. For example, as of tomorrow, people in New York will be restricted in how sugary their drinks can be. Yeah, America is full of fat people who need to watch portion control, but denying someone a Double Double just because other people can't keep themselves healthy is bullshit. They even mentioned potential laws regarding headphones and how loud you can have them. Seriously? What in the fuck gives law-makers the right to tell you to turn your music down? As a devout music fan, I find this to be an invasion of simple human rights. And it is not necessarily just these few laws that make me wonder, it's what they will come up with next that really scares me. As a Canadian, I doubt we will see any effect from these laws, not anytime soon at least. But seriously, you can go buy fuckloads of booze and cigarettes, and all that the government is concerned about is how sugary your morning coffee is. Seriously, gtfo.

Ignorance is a pandemic. Contradictions and hypocrisy run rampant. Let the obese people have their 32 ounce big gulps from 7/11 and start to, I dunno, worry about why no one can get a job, why the economy is crashing, and why America has so many gun-related homicides. I am not saying I know all there is to know about politics, or even the USA, but I know a lot about common sense. Common sense is an endangered species, for lack of a better term. I weep for the future and am glad that I will most likely not be around to see the real collapse of common sense.

I watch TV and all I see are commercials about hair loss, make-up, white teeth, deodorant that will apparently get you laid, and weight loss 'innovations'. No wonder self-esteem is at an all-time low. Yellow teeth? Overweight? Good luck getting a date. At least that is the message sent by the media. It reminds me of Michael Moore's interview about Columbine with Manson... He says the media is centred around fear, and that is one of the truest statements I have ever heard.

I could ramble on about this forever, but I think I have made my point.

World.... Just.... *Facepalm*

- XV

The Following
March 11th, 2013

Television has really gone to shit these days with 'reality' shows like Duck Dynasty, that annoying fat kid Honey Boo Boo, and pretty much every show on TLC. However, it seems that one show has finally embraced what I believe we need to see more of on TV - a truly twisted show. The Following is relentless and shows the extremes of the violent side of the human psyche. Sure, we normally would root for the protagonist, played by Kevin Bacon (you may remember seeing his dick in Hollow Man), but personally I root for this cult. To be shocking, to be ruthless, and to be faithful to the cause. In my twisted little mind, I enjoy the sick and twisted nature of the show. Clearly it's popular, and that's because people want to see violence, and they will deny that to their graves. Inside all of us is a part that wants to see the hero get a knife in the chest, maybe see an innocent victim tortured. Inside all of us is darkness, just as there is light. For the most part, people will ignore the dark, pretend it is not there, and even fight to keep the dark deep, deep inside. That is why people like me, who accept the dark, who admit it exists, and even embraces it are seen as 'abnormal' in society. Who's more abnormal, the person who wears masks and lies to themselves and others about their darker thoughts, or the person who accepts the dark as a part of human nature and does not run from it?

Obviously I am not trying to promote murderous cults based on a literary genius, nor violence in general. All I am saying is that people need to accept the duality of their nature. That only a thin line separates a Saint from a Serial Killer. Take off the masks you wear, take a deeper look inside. You might just like what you find... Unless that concept frightens you?

In other news, I am still battling a particularly heavy depression, seemingly idiopathic, but somewhat normal for me nonetheless. I am not eating, I am (for once) over-sleeping, not getting outside (unless I need a cigarette), and isolating myself from what few people I have left in my life. I still have to wait over 3 weeks to see the psychiatrist, who will undoubtedly listen to me for two minutes, give me some random medication to add to my collection, and push me out the door. It's a new age in psychiatry, with the long-winded title of 'Let's Ignore Patient's Problems And Instead Cover It Up With A Band-Aid Prescription So We Do Not Have To Face Reality'.... or of course 'LIPPAICIUWABAPSWDNHTFR' for short. Sure seems to be working for those billionaire CEO's of the Pharmaceutical industry. Screw the patients, amiright?

- XV

Further Down the Rabbit Hole
March 12th, 2013

Getting out of bed was a monumental task today, more so than usual. I woke up lethargic and weak. I still have a lot of trouble falling asleep, but now I have trouble getting back up again. It was past noon by the time I could drag myself out from under the covers and feebly stand up. No breakfast, just a glass of water and a cigarette. Then a walk to the pharmacy to get all of my meds, i knew today would be a Xanax day, so I forced myself to make the trek... not that it's all that far, but when you feel like I do, it may as well be miles away.

I am trying to channel some of my depression and angst into music. This involves a mix of listening to Marilyn Manson, as well as trying to write some stuff myself. I have most of a song written, now all I need is a decent singing voice. But I am not in it for the infinitesimal possibility that I will become famous one day... that, my friends, is a delusion. Then again, reality has not been too kind to me, so maybe I can find solace in delusions.

I just want things to be different. I want to see a doctor who actually gives a fuck, who listens and can at least make some difference in my mood and sleep. I have been bounced back and forth like a fucking ping pong ball from doctor to doctor, diagnosis to diagnosis, and medication to medication. No wonder I am addicted to drugs, they seem to be the only thing that works (even just temporarily) and the only constant in my life. It's amazing what power they have to lift you out of the darkest hole. I am not so delusional to think it is a permanent fix, but fuck, I'll take that over the massive amounts of legal medications that do nothing. As a Canadian, I used to brag about the Medical system in Canada, but frankly, it fucking sucks for someone in my position. You can find psychiatrists to peddle medications, but good luck finding one that will spend more than 5 minutes with you. I always leave their offices feeling worse and more helpless than before. Xanax takes the edge off the crippling anxiety, Seroquil makes it a bit easier to sleep, but the Prozac might as well be a placebo. Three years on this medication and things have only gotten worse. Now I know I cannot expect meds to be the only solution, but I have tried all kinds of therapy and frankly, it has not worked. Besides, therapists are a bitch to find unless you can spare $100 a week... Which I most definitely cannot.

So I remain stuck. As usual.

- XV

A Glimmer On The Horizon, Or Another Let-Down?
March 12th, 2013

Having multiple mental disorders requires multiple medications. Suffice it to say, I have tried almost every medication under the Sun, whether prescribed for me or not. I was going to try to make a list on here, but my memory fails me, and I would have to skim through almost 700 pages of my written journals. Maybe that will be my task tomorrow. But I digress. My friend told me he had recently switched to a medication called Wellbutrin. I have heard of it, but seeing as my doctor is a saggy fucker that should have retired when disco was in, I never had the chance to try it. He seemed to think keeping me on the Prozac was best, I mean, I've been on it for 3 years, it has GOTTA kick in soon right? Wrong. So April 4th I see an actual real psychologist, but as my last posts have hinted, I have little faith in our medical system. Especially when it is related to mental health. Anyway, Wellbutrin is supposed to have fewer side-effects, work faster and better, and have anti-anxiety benefits as well as a slight boost of energy to counteract my hypersomnia. I am not throwing all my chips in at once over this possible medication, but it has been the only ray of hope since my doctor realized Xanax would benefit me.

The pessimist in me, however, remembers the dozens of failed medications and horrible side-effects ranging from dry-mouth to full on psychosis. This should be fun. I will not leave this doctor's office until he listens to me and gives me the new medication. if he says no, look for a hostage situation on the news April 4th. That will be me. Snapping.

- XV

An Insomniac's Lament
March 13th, 2013

Falling asleep should be fucking simple. Lay down, close your eyes, and let sleep happen. But no. Not for me. For me, I must take borderline lethal doses of various medications just to have a chance to sleep. After hours of tossing, turning, and swearing in frustration, I fall into a non-restorative, light sleep. I wake up several times during the night and morning until finally trying to drag my ass out of bed around noon. Once in a while I can see this as being normal, but every fucking night drives you mad. It drains you, frustrates you, and makes a normal night's sleep seem hopeless. So here I am, tired and angry, rambling about my lack of sleep. Fuck you, Sandman. Why do you skip my bed?

- XV

(no subject)
March 14th, 2013

Total brain block today. Maybe it's from increasing my meds more and more every day. Too tired, too bleh. Fuck you life.

- XV

The Dark Passenger
March 15th, 2013

The Dark Passenger (from the series *Dexter*) is a concept I find to be quite interesting and accurate. Inside all of us is a Demon, the voice telling you to do the wrong thing, to fuck shit up, and to make you lose control. This is what the Dark Passenger is. While most people find it quite easy to control this, other fight and fight, and some end up losing. I have fought this Passenger through my relationships as well as my drug addiction. It will always be there, telling me I want more, telling me to press the big red button that says 'Do not push!'. Once in a while, however, I find it is important to let the Passenger take the wheel and see what happens. Ignoring it only makes things worse. Come to your own conclusions about what you think the Dark Passenger is, and how it has affected you.

You will be hearing more about mine in the near future.

- XV

The Dark Passenger II
March 15th, 2013

This concept of the Dark Passenger intrigues me. Specifically my battle to keep it down, to stop it from manifesting for others to see. I know what goes on in my head, what I do that no one sees, the temptations never fulfilled. Eventually the dam is going to burst. With every bit of stress, every sleepless night, and every day feeling empty and worthless, the Dark Passenger grows stronger and gains more influence on my life. I had not cut since June, when I needed 30 stitches. After that, it seemed pointless. Suddenly, I was at it again. Not to the extent of the June incident, but enough to make me question my sanity. Now I realize it is not just me that is going crazy, that is falling... I am being pushed and pulled, contorted in every direction by this Passenger. He has taken up residence in my mind and slowly his poisons are seeping into my veins.

I feel too sick to eat, too exhausted to sleep (make sense of that one...) , and too empty to do anything about it. I thought I had at least one person to count on. I do not want to be someone's burden. No one deserves that. But the more I sit alone, isolated, the darker things get and the looser my grip on reality becomes.

What light that is left in me is being snuffed out by The Dark Passenger. Maybe he knows what I really want.

PS. A special thanks to my father (who **totally** is not an alcoholic) for ditching our plans once again to go drink with your buddies. Call me an addict, I call you a fucking hypocrite. Have fun passing out every night with a bottle of whiskey.

- XV

The Dark Passenger III
March 15th, 2013

Yeah, three posts about the same thing. But this way of looking at my life has made things so much clearer. Sometimes I let the Dark Passenger 'take the wheel' for a while, which usually coincides with my coke-snorting, MDMA-popping, and other self-injurious activities. To keep it caged up would be suicide. When it gets out, all Hell would break loose. I try to maintain a balance between light and dark, but lately the light has become more and more feeble.

I chase the light away, because the dark fits better.

I do not mean in the emo 'I'm so fucking troubled, please pay attention to me' way, I mean in the 'I do not give a shit anymore, let the dark do what it wants'. I have spent years fighting the Dark Passenger for control, and I grow weary of the constant battle between 'right' and 'wrong'. Who the fuck decided that anyway? I guess it is the select few, the governmental elite, that decide whether or not something is 'acceptable'.

I feel like the Greek king Sisyphus, damned to a lifetime of pushing an immense boulder up a hill, only to have it fall back down as I reach the top. Perpetually stuck, repeating the same old shit, over and over. People tell me that one of these days the boulder will stay at the top of the hill, but I doubt it. I know gravity, and gravity is a bitch. Just ask that coyote on the cartoons that always falls off a cliff. It also seems the more I fight it, or try to make things better, more weight is added to the boulder. Even more weight is added with every sleepless night and tortured thought.

I have battled depression and related symptoms for years now. I'm sick and tired of being sick and tired. I have tried in the past to throw in the towel, but something is keeping me here. Do I really believe at the end of all this is a light? That I will be rewarded for my suffering? Fuck no. I cannot honestly say that I have any idea what my future holds. I can no longer see one. Everything is changing constantly and just when I think I may have something figured out, I don't.

So why try? For the naive hope that maybe someday things will get better? I would rather expect nothing and not be disappointed. Yes, call that pessimism.

The Silent Observer has been a little too silent.

- XV

Autopsy
March 16th, 2013

I had a dream last night. I was on a metal table with bright lights shining down on me. No, it was not an extraterrestrial experience. I realized a man wearing a mask was cutting a large incision down the length of my stomach. He peeled back the skin and grabbed something from his table. It was some type of saw, and made the most horrible screeching sound as it cut through my sternum. I could hear him crack my ribs open. He was looking down at my corpse with shock. I was empty. No organs, no blood, no guts... nothing. After that it all gets foggy.

Being such a shitty sleeper, my dreams are often interrupted by my body's random need to wake up sweating at 5:30 am. You would have to be a bona-fide moron to not understand the symbolism behind my empty body.

Anyway, back to real life. I still feel like I am being dragged downwards. Tonight I may let my Dark Passenger take the wheel for fun. I have been holding it back so long I no longer see the point.

Moar later.

- XV

Lethargy
March 17th, 2013

I spent most of the day in bed. It wasn't even because I was hung over from last night, I just had no motivation. My back is sore, my head is pounding, my limbs are as limp as an old man's dick, and I am fighting just to concentrate on typing.

It's St. Patrick's Day. Do I give a fuck? Like we, especially the Irish, need a holiday in which to drink our faces off and puke up green beer all night.

It is really hard to form a thought right now, let alone type. Maybe tomorrow I will have more interesting things to say... I doubt it.

Drive safe, Snickerdoodle

- XV

Pain's Not Ashamed To Repeat Itself
March 18th, 2013

This cycle needs to end. I need something different, something new. The same old shit just isn't working for me anymore. But what the fuck can I do? I have stuck myself between a rock and a hard place and it's crushing in on me more and more each day. My Dark Passenger is screaming its desires. It wants a life for me that I cannot sustain. If he takes the wheel, all Hell will break loose. A flurry of blood, drugs, and self-mutilation will become my life. We don't want that now do we?

Do we?

- XV

Hurt
March 18th, 2013

How much hurt can one endure? At what point do they finally break from the pressure and the pain? Would that be the true measure of a man? Everyone reaches a breaking point, the only difference is how we react. Some yell into a pillow, others may go as far as murder. For me, I seem to have several breaking points, and most of them have already been broken. I am reaching another breaking point. This lethargy and insomnia is consuming me, literally eating away at me. I'm sure there are Ethiopians with better diets than I have.

So I ask again, how much hurt can one endure?

I think we may find out sooner rather than later.

- XV

Arma-Goddamn-Motherfuckin-Geddon
March 19th, 2013

"Last night I dreamt of the apocalypse. The rivers ran red with blood, fire rained down from the sky setting the world ablaze, and demons were exterminating anyone they saw. I remember a child, green eyes, lost and alone, enveloped by Hellfire, burn away to ashes. I watched as the city before me crumbled and burned. I realized I was standing on a large hill overlooking the city. I realized I was not scared. I realized I had done this. I was smiling. God could not hear their cries for help, even if He could, it was too late, even for God. Beside me were 15 demons, each with 'XV' etched into their decaying skin, right over where a heart should be but only darkness is found. This was my army. Eventually, what was not covered in blood was coated with ashes. A city reduced to rubble. I realized what city it was. It was Jerusalem. What once stood as a mighty symbol of religious beliefs and beginnings was now gone."

Then I woke up. No idea why, or what the fuck the dream was all about, but it was incredibly lucid. I don't *hate* religion, I just fail to see the point of it. I won't get down on my knees and pray to a God that will send you to Hell for eternity if you sin. Look at the world... Where is God now? It's as if there is a sign on the Pearly Gates saying "Be Back Soon", like you see at some stores. I have tried to believe in something. An ex of mine was a devout Christian, I could just never understand it. I found it to be foolish for me to keep talking to myself and hoping things get better. God, I tried, I just got your voicemail... again. Your inbox is full, bro.

Blasphemous, I know. I respect other people's beliefs and ideals **only** as long as they respect my beliefs too, however negative or smart-assed they are. I see no point. If you cannot find the strength within yourself to make life better, what do you think praying is gonna do? I know, I sound like a hypocrite, considering I have a dark and generally dreary view of myself and the world, but let the record show I must play Devil's Advocate here.

"I'm not a slave to a God
  that doesn't exist
And I'm not a slave to a world
  that doesn't give a shit."
- The Fight Song - Marilyn Manson

- XV

Into Pieces (Featuring the Incredible Hulk)
March 20th, 2013

I feel like I am slowly falling apart. Sleep is always a fucking adventure for me. It's never simple, like it should be. I average about 3 hours of decent sleep per night, and have adapted somewhat to that lack of sleep. Anyone else would be crippled after a day or two of this low level of sleep, but I have no choice but to evolve. I am in a lot of pain. My muscles are beaten and fatigued, making it nearly impossible to do anything. Not that I have all kinds of shit to do, but this lack of energy is killing me, very, very slowly. Maybe I don't mind, maybe I've accepted my circumstances as well as my fate. I do not live each day like it's my last, I just try to get through the day with all the bullshit I have been 'blessed' with. Another reason I do not believe in God, btw. If He exists, He is an asshole.

I keep having fucked up dreams. Last night I was with a group of random people, including an ex I haven't talked to in years, and we all seemed to have special abilities, like the movie Chronicle. We were levitating and flying around, but as time passed, the abilities started to fade. I got all panicky and tried to warn the rest of the people that it would wear off. I found the group and for some reason I will never understand, they all turned into the Hulk... Yes, the Incredible Hulk. They starting fighting each other as I was running through the crowd power-punching Hulks left and right. I escaped the chaos of several dozen Hulks with my ex. I had just enough power to fly away to safety. After that it gets blurry, but I'm pretty sure Freud would have a field-day with what happened next.

I found one of my old belts yesterday and tried it on. I bought it when I was using coke nearly every day, and I had to make new holes so I could tighten the belt more. But now it's a bit different. Still fits, but I don't need the holes I made anymore. I miss my coke diet, as unhealthy as it was.

-XV

Lips Like Morphine
March 20th, 2013

*"I want a girl with lips like morphine
Knock me out every time they touch me
I wanna feel that kiss just crush me
And break me down"*

- Lips Like Morphine - Kill Hannah

Not literally, although that would be a nice bonus. How is someone like me supposed to find someone? Someone who can see past my mental illnesses, past the scars lining my arms and chest, past the darkness and into the shrinking flicker of light. I have learned getting into a relationship is like pulling the pin on a grenade. It always blows up and leaves both in pieces. Even if I found someone, can I ask them to bear my burdens? Can I ask them to bear with me while I self-destruct? The simple, and most obvious answer is no. Will I ever be 'normal'... Fuck no. Do I want to be? Fuck no. It would be nice, however to have someone who gets me, who accepts both my good side as well as my Dark Passenger. The real question is if my Dark Passenger will allow me to find someone, and hold onto them without destroying the both of us.

Maybe I can't get a girl with lips like morphine... But I will certainly settle for just morphine.

- XV

Something Wicked This Way Comes
March 20th, 2013

Yes, please ignore the nerdy reference. I can feel it in my bones. My body has never been so weak, my mind has never been so out of control. Control has always been my nemesis, and now it seems that I have lost the fight. All I have to look forward to is **another** psychiatrist appointment, **another** battery of tests and depression inventories, and **another** batch of new medications that may or may not fuck me up even more. Apparently I have 40 minutes with this doctor, almost unheard of at this place. Usually you cannot even get a sentence in and you are whisked out the door like a shitty diaper. This cycle I have been caught in with the medical system needs to end. It is wearing me down to nothing. I am not much to begin with.

My Dark Passenger does not like the idea of new medications. He would rather me be back on cocaine and MDMA benders, because however synthetic and temporary the relief is, it is more than any prescription has ever done. I know it, and he knows it. Where to go from here seems like an impossible question. I have no choice but to live day to day. Every day that I don't snap is a success to me. My Passenger wants, even craves, chaos. I have given him plenty, and I am sure there is plenty more to come. It's a gut feeling, but mine are usually pretty accurate. If history has taught me anything, it is that the past is the best predictor of the future. If that is as true as I think it is, shit is really about to hit the fan.

It is not pessimism, but observation. I wish I am wrong. I wish I could sleep, be happy, take off the mask and be human again. I can barely look at myself in the mirror anymore. I am wasting away. I am not sure if I care or not.

- XV

Crash
March 21st, 2013

From the amount of shit I have put my body through, I should be dead, or close to it. But still I test its limits with substance and all around self-injurious behaviour. I have been mentioning that my body is growing weaker, but this is a whole new low. It's only a matter of time before I crash and burn. Do I care? Nahh. Should I? Depends who you ask. If you are an optimist, I suggest you do not ask.

- XV

Unkillable Monster
March 22nd, 2013

I know I sounded weak tonight. I sounded pessimistic and hopeless, but it's all I know. I always say that history is the best tool to predict the future. You know me all too well, but there are some things I keep close to the chest. There are some secrets I need to keep just because they would make no difference. When I think of relationships, I think of pain, heartbreak, self-destruction, and the feeling of being completely alone. In that way, I am weak. In my mind, no one deserves the pain I can cause. The pain I have caused countless times before. I should probably sew my mouth shut and break off my fingers, lest I ruin yet another beautiful thing.

I have gotten good at putting on my brave face and pretending I do not mind being alone. In actuality, it's dehumanizing me more each day. The further I put myself from people, the safer they are, but the more broken I become. No one should have to pick up the pieces. What would be the point?

I feel like the great destroyer, an Unkillable Monster, wreaking havoc wherever I go. It is like a shitty form of the Midas Touch, where everything I come into contact with is blown to pieces.

"How the fuck are we supposed to know
When I'm a monster, with the way
You refuse to die
How the fuck are we supposed to know
If we're in love
Or if we're in pain

I'm a tightrope walker
I can't find my circus
And I'm damaged beyond repair
You're just a coffin
Of a girl I knew
And I'm buried in you

You never said "I'll end up like this"
No. No, no, no

Sometimes I dream I'm an exterminating angel
A traveling executioner from heaven
Sometimes I dream I'm an exterminating angel
A traveling executioner from heaven
Sent to give you the prettiest death I know
Call the grave and make our reservations

You never said "I'll end up like this"
No!
You never said "I'll end up like this"
No, no, no, no
Are we in love or are we in pain?

Why is my wound a front door to you?
Am I my own shadow?"

- Unkillable Monster - Marilyn Manson

- XV

Meaning
March 23rd, 2013

I have searched in vain for my meaning in life, if one exists. I thought I could be a lot of things, do a lot of things, but clearly they weren't meant to be. Everyone tries to find meaning in their lives, and some are successful. I'm starting to think that maybe I don't have a meaning, and maybe that's how it's meant to be. Or maybe I have found my meaning already. That would be true if my meaning was to be a drug addict/university drop-out/heartbreaker.

It's hard to make sense of all the chaos I have faced and created. It's like looking at a thousand puzzle pieces and trying to see what it makes. Except pieces are missing, and some aren't even from that puzzle. I'm not sure we are meant to know what our meaning truly is. Or maybe there is no meaning at all.

- XV

Substance (...And The Comedown)
March 24th, 2013

Another night of reckless substance abuse. For the night, I was able to forget my problems and my pain. For a while I was free from the burden of my sickness. Sure, you can argue that substance is not the answer, but to be honest, sometimes it is. Sometimes you need that vacation, that time away from real life where you can forget. Where beer takes over and makes everything okay, for a while. Sure, it is temporary, and once this high is gone, I am back to my misery. But a night of recklessness was exactly what I needed. A dose of that special powder was long overdue.

Substance can make or break someone. For some, it controls their lives. Every thought is about the next high. That used to be me. But now, I can go without and be fine. That doesn't mean, however, that when the opportunity arises I will say no. I seem to have a problem with impulse control. It's part of my illness, and I am learning to live with it. It is my 'cross to bear'. I used to be consumed by substance, by the numb, by the escape, and by the high. Now I have learned moderation is the key. Maybe I will always be an addict, but it will no longer define or control me.

As someone who used to use drugs (coke, morphine, etc) on a regular basis, I am actually shocked by my control over what was once something that controlled my life. I would always fear the comedown, when the drugs no longer mask the pain and I am forced to face reality once again. That part is never fun, but the Xanax sure helps. Recently I have had the ability to be free from the cravings. Why I have been able to do this is still a mystery to me, but I am glad I have some sort of control. My Dark Passenger sometimes gets the best of me, but hey, I am only human.... I think.

The high is something I miss. But it ruined my life, and it's about time I grow up and face this illness head-on. Shit is gonna change. Shit is gonna get real. Shit is gonna no longer control me. I don't need some higher power to beg for mercy to. I will do this myself. What choice do I have?

- XV

Distance
March 26th, 2013

One thing I pride myself in is being able to keep distance between myself and others. It is this barrier that stops me from destroying something innocent, something good. The space is for people's own good. Recently faced with an issue of closeness, I experienced a pretty heavy anxiety attack. It was not so much fear of the situation, but fear of what I could do. I need to stay away, before the blood flows and hearts break. Will I ever get over this fear of destroying people? Or is it just a rationalization created to deal with my social phobia? Either way, the end seems to always be the same... Pain.

"So turn around, walk away
Before you confuse the way we abuse each other
If you're not afraid of getting hurt
Then I'm not afraid of how much I hurt you

I'm well aware I'm a danger to my self
Are you aware I'm a danger to others?
There's a crack in my soul
You thought was a smile"

- Leave A Scar, Marilyn Manson

Looks can be deceiving, and behaviour even more so. Sure, I know how to act the part in most situations, but eventually someone will see through my lies.

In other news, I am having doubts about seeing this psychiatrist. Over the last 4 years, I have seen about a dozen different psychiatrists, and no one was able to figure out what was wrong with me. Now with my diagnosis of BPD, maybe it will be easier to treat. Still, I have my trepidations about what the outcome will be. Will he actually listen? Will he just throw more prescriptions at me? Sometimes I hope the latter would be the case. I have given up faith in the medical system. They bounce me back and forth like a fucking tennis ball. If the doctor just wants to mask everything with medications, that is fine with me. It's what I do with drugs anyways. I just have to make sure the dose is high enough to keep reality from giving me a reach-around.

- XV

The Dark Passenger IV - The Poisonous Self
March 26th, 2013

Continuing my "Dark Passenger" series, I find myself faced with an impossible situation. The situation needs no explanation, just because it doesn't fucking matter. All I know is that I need to stop this person. She is playing Russian Roulette with a full clip. She has no idea the devastation I have caused, and will cause. That will be dealt with as I usually deal with things - a distant indifference, with undertones of self-mutilation and drug use. No denying my Dark Passenger everything he asks for. Once in a while, depravity wins. Once in a while a flicker of evil crosses my mind. I know the right thing to do. The way it should be, and should always be. It's not me giving up on relationships, it's me accepting I am poisonous.

It may be time for the mask to come off, before this goes any further. Before my Dark Passenger gains any more control over me. I just don't know what the fuck to do. Every decision leaves someone fucking hurt, as it always has. I would much rather it be my blood spilled than anyone else's. I know what I **should** do, but if you've read this far, you know me better than that. Odds are I will take it as far as it can go before exploding and watch as it teeters on the ledge.

No amount of Xanax and cigarettes can make this easier. As usual, I am forced to face my Demons head on. They will win eventually.

- XV

Hindsight
March 27th, 2013

Just one day until I turn 23. Looking back on the year that just passed, let alone the last 4 years, is (for lack of a better term) disturbing. I thought I would be different, I thought I would have done something worth writing about. All I did was take a year and continue fucking up everything I touch. I have spent thousands of dollars on drugs, booze, and cigarettes to numb myself. Now? Now I am broke, depressed, medicated, and all around shitty. Where will I be one year from now? Probably in the same position.

People say hindsight is 20/20, but that doesn't mean shit when you don't do anything about it. Same goes for potential. Just as pointless unless you give enough of a fuck to use it. Hindsight for me is a horror show, filled with pain and suffering. Memories of people in the past I loved, lost, and buried. People who said they cared but proved that they truly didn't give a fuck. I guess that is one change I have made. Isolating myself from people in general, as opposed to getting fucked in the ass by their lies and betrayals.

To be honest, I am shocked I made it through the year. Two suicide attempts (or something like a suicide attempt) have left me scarred, weak, and empty. I would love to be optimistic about this coming year, that maybe I will be writing a much happier story, but the fact is, that is not my life. I have accepted my place in the Universe and despite bitching about it from time to time, I have no choice but to adapt. Darwin was right,

- XV

Going Nowhere Fast
March 27th, 2013

I really am growing weary of sitting around day after day. I say it not for pity, but because it's true. Everyone is the fucking expert suddenly when it comes to my illness. They have all the advice in the world but not one smidgen of evidence to back it up. I swear, if I hear 'Why don't you go out and do something?' one more time, I will fucking snap. I barely have the energy to drag my ass out of bed, let alone wander around town looking for activities to fill my time.

I am falling apart, not just mentally, but physically. I had to stop writing this post so I could go vomit. Seriously. All this shit is piling on and my body seems to be throwing in the towel. I have some fight left in me, but something needs to change. At the same time I am afraid to move forward because I fear the unknown. The future to me is shapeless and grey. Going through all the shit I am, my parents are still hounding me to figure out what I want to do with my life. **I don't fucking know!** It almost seems like they think I enjoy this lifestyle, or whatever the fuck this 'life' is. Yes, I love feeling perpetually worthless, empty, depressed, and anxious. I love not having any friends or relationships. I loooove all the pill bottles littering my room. I love the stigma, oh and especially the scars. Seriously? SERIOUSLY? Seriously.

I am putting all the fight I have left in to make it to this psychiatrist appointment on April 4th. Eight days seems like an eternity. I am also setting myself up for a potential upset. If I go in there and hear another doctor tell me they don't know what to do with me, I will completely lose any hope or drive I have left. It sounds ridiculous putting all my chips on this doctor, but after seeing more than a dozen 'professionals', it's about time I get one that can tell me what the fuck is going on, as well as what medication and therapies to be taking. I will not take no for an answer from this doctor. I will not move out of that fucking chair until he helps me. Until security comes, of course.

Then my Passenger nags one question, over and over, into my head - *'Can you even be helped? Are some people just beyond repair?'*. He has a point. After so many different diagnoses, therapies, medications, and shit in my life, there must be a point of no return. How close I am to it is something I don't know, and probably don't want to know.

- XV

Happy Birthday to Me
March 28th, 2013

I look back at my 'legacy'; a summation of my choices and actions in my life. I see shit. Pure shit. I should be that person I was years ago when I went off to Queen's University, endless possibilities at my feet. Now, I am a drop-out with copious amounts of debt, mental illness, and all-around shittyness.

My birthday is just another day to me, I see no reason to celebrate the anniversary of the day I was pushed out of the womb. If anything, my Mom should get gifts, not me. But our consumerist society has turned every occasion into a spending money occasion. I do not want any gifts, if anything, I would just like to be with people I care about. I don't care about presents.
Well it's midnight. Officially one year older... Hurrah?

- XV

XV
March 28th, 2013

"If you can hear this don't assume that I'm talking to you
Yesterday everything I thought I believed in died but today is my
birthday
Today is my birthday
I don't need you, I'll say it to myself
It doesn't mean I won't need somebody
Anyone with half a soul will hear this and will never leave me

If you don't know what forever feels like
I'll show you what it feels like with out it

This time I won't hesitate to kill to protect what I believe in
This time I won't hesitate to kill to protect what I believe in

I get by now I'm not really dead
But I really needed someone to save me
Leaving me alone to die
Is worse than having the guts to kill me

If you don't know what forever feels like
I'll show you what it feels like with out it
I'll show you what it feels like without it

This time I won't hesitate to kill to protect what I believe in

Not letting you in
Won't satisfy me
I'll teach you about loss"

- 15 - Marilyn Manson

- XV

Not In the State
March 30th, 2013

To write anything, I mean. Substance wins this round. More later.

- XV

Occam's Razor, Etc.
April 1st, 2013

So for the last few days I have been testing a new sleep routine... And because of the obviousness of this solution, I have named this entry accordingly. Weed. Yep, the 'socially acceptable' street drug. It, along with my other meds has greatly shortened how long it takes me to fall asleep, and my ability to remain asleep. The simplest solution is the obvious solution. It works... for now.

Only in Canada can you be, one day, drinking cold beer on the back deck with the sun baking you from the insides, to the next day, where flurries are being tossed around by cold winds. Only in Canada.

I just want to say to a close friend going through a rough time: Prioritize, realize, look forward, and decide if you are where you want to be. You will find your way, Snickerdoodle.

- XV

D-Day
April 4th, 2013

This is it. The big day. The deciding factor for my future. I have 40 minutes to explain to this psychiatrist why he should take my case, because he literally is the last one in the area. I've tried others and they have been fails. Epic fails. Hence the trepidation I have for this appointment. Everything needs to change. My meds no longer work.

Will have to update. Though I guess I can argue that I have tried these meds for THREE FUCKING YEARS! and nothing! No change, if anything, it's only gotten worse.

If he is unable to have me as a patient, or sends me back to my family doctor, this may be my last entry. Everything I have, everything I am is riding on this appointment. Or am I making a mountain out of a molehill?

- XV

And So It Begins
April 4th, 2013

I was half an hour early for my appointment today, despite being sick and fucked up on cough syrup. I still had to wait over a fucking HOUR to see this doctor. He told me to stop being a druggie, then continued to write 4 new prescriptions for me (one doubled the dose of one of my meds).

See you in two weeks, doc. I made it clear he was my last chance to get consistent care from a psychiatrist, and I felt he saw my desperation. He said he will help me out, if I help myself out by staying clean and seeing a councillor.

This has been one fucked up day, just in general. Like how I'm feeling. And I do not feel like typing.... so...

- XV

In Coma
April 5th, 2013

Well let me begin by saying a big 'holy shit' to the doctor I saw yesterday. The new meds, as well as the one he doubled, knocked me out cold. That's usually good for an insomniac, but I have spent most of the day in bed, too tired to do anything. These meds are kicking my ass. I'm sure I will get used to them in a few days, but maybe this is what I need... A couple of days in bed to 'recover'. I am still staying clean, and despite the bitchings of my Dark Passenger, I intend to stay clean for a while. It will take time to wean off my old meds and let the new ones work, so for the next few weeks it is pretty much a waiting game to see if they will help me or destroy me.

Due to these new medications, I cannot say that I will continue my daily entries in here. Until I find more energy, LJ may have to take a backseat.

- XV

<u>Nostalgia</u>
April 8th, 2013

I miss the life I once had, years ago, before the diagnosis, before the pills, before the cutting and cocaine. Times seem simpler in hindsight. High school was both a bitch and good at times too. Reckless partying into the wee hours of the morning, bottle in one hand, a girl in the other. Blackout drunk nights, school drama, summer vacations and flings. It feels like I have already passed the climax of my life, and now, I just rot away from drugs and sickness. Years ago I was a different person. Carefree, looking forward to university... I just wish someone would have warned me that I would turn out like this. I have issues when it comes to clinging onto the past. I start to miss the people, the parties, and a life not defined by mental illness.

But that was then, and this is now. It would be a misjudgement to call what I have now a life. I feel no life, I live no life. Just a rotting corpse with only nostalgia and substance to get through the day.

- XV

Disposable (Teens)
April 10th, 2013

Sick... Don't know if it's withdrawals, the new meds, or just allergies. All I know is I am out of patience. Seems I am disposable, just as is the proverbial leper. Why? It's the way I am, I suppose. Ponder on that, for just a little bit.

- X-fuckin-V

The Return
April 20th, 2013

My neglect of this journal is obvious. For the last few weeks I have been sick as fuck with bronchitis. The only good thing to come from it was a prescription for cough medicine with codeine. Good times. Suffice it to say not much has really happened in the few weeks I was out of commission. Just a whole lot of nothing.

As the bronchitis wears off, I will continue business as usual. Not that I was missed.

- XV

The Golden Age of Grotesque

April 23rd, 2013

"We're the low art Gloominati, and we aim to depress
The scabaret sacrilegends
This is the Golden Age of Grotesque"
-GAOG - MM

It seems like America, and even Canada, is under attack. Bombings, explosions, poison mail, floods, terror plots... All in the last two weeks. Maybe it's a sign of the times. I do not believe in coincidences. Everything is linked, which makes sense if you understand the Law of Large Numbers. Being the pessimist that I am, I would bet that it is only going to get worse. Maybe if America didn't piss so many people off.... Just saying...

For me, I am in a state of transition. Moving, new opportunities, and even a new life clean (for the most part) off drugs. I try not to get my hopes up, seeing as the last several years have shared the same theme - disappointment and self-destruction. I will admit, a sober life is not as good as a drugged-up life. Despite all the problems drugs caused me, I will always be an addict. Even if I do not crave cocaine or MDMA, there will always be a voice in the back of my head (my Dark Passenger) taunting and teasing, working towards a relapse. I am not naive enough to say I am done with substances, however. I believe that this sobriety and slightly more positive outlook is a phase. It is not a question of 'if', it is a question of 'when'.

More later.

- XV

Birthday
April 25th, 2013

This will be one of the few posts where I get sentimental. Today is my brother's birthday. Since I was young, he has always been someone I looked up to, and we have always been close. He has gone through similar problems as me with drugs and recklessness, but he turned his life around and joined the military. Now he is moving up through the ranks and making me proud to be his brother.

Happy birthday, bro!

- XV

Leaving Me Alone to Die Is Worse Than Having the Guts to Kill Me
April 30th, 2013

Excuses, excuses. Yeah, that was me then, and clearly you don't give a fuck about me now. So I say get off your fucking high-horse and realize that you are not much different from me. I still remember the nights of cocaine and sex. You are a goddamn hypocrite. Sure, I fucked up. It's in my nature. But so did you. What makes you think that you are so different? So fucking Christian and perfect?

You said you were protecting yourself. Did you give a fuck about me? Oh, and the smug fucking comment you made "You're still holding resentment against me?" Fuck yeah! After 14 years of knowing each other, you walk away without even a "See you later" and you are shocked? To be honest, I am clearly not the only one holding a grudge. I wish nothing but pain and suffering for you and your loved ones.

- XV

... And All Things Will End
May 1st, 2013

... More or less.

I thought I was done with substance for now, but fuck was I proven wrong. I am not ready to let this feeling go. Sure, it's not "socially acceptable", but when have I ever done something that is? Exxxaccttllyyyy.

Fuck it, people can say what they want, make their own decisions about who I am. I really do not give even a *single* fuck. Not even close. Then again, when have I? Exactly.

All things will end. Story of my life. So many doors have been shut on my face that I have lost count. People just give up, they lose the feelings they claim that they had. I have learned a valuable lesson to not let myself get burned like that again. Sure it makes for a rather lonely life, but at least I won't be shit on again.

- XV

Murderers Are Getting Prettier Every Day
May 5th, 2013

I fucked up. I think you can figure out what I did. It's what I always do to hide the pain and misery. To escape from the monotonous drag of my life. I honestly do not even feel bad. It's part of who I am. Besides, I am not hurting anyone, am I? Maybe just myself, but that is MY choice. I am not going to change into the person everyone wants me to be. The pressure I had in high school was immeasurable. As the youngest, the standards were higher for me, maybe that was because my brother was not doing as well as he is now. I had to get top marks, go to university, become a doctor, and not fuck up. I was on my way, but something happened, and I believe it was inevitable. For years I have been told I am sick, mentally ill, an addict throwing my life away. Well fuck, if you do not like who I am, then stop wasting your time trying to mould me into something I am not. I do not apologize for how I am. I am a product of this fucked up generation.

- XV

This Can't Be Right
May 6th, 2013

Something is wrong with the force. I don't feel like myself. Maybe I am turning into something I am not supposed to be. Maybe the pressures from family and friends is getting to me. I always knew that "The boy that you loved is the man that you fear" would pretty much sum me up. Up until recently I was on track for that. Sobriety has made me dull and lifeless. No more euphoria, no more energy, no more reckless abuse of my body. Funny how I miss that... Well, not really. But I do. I take solace in the fact that this is just temporary. Until next time...

- XV

Mutilation Is the Most Sincere Form Of Flattery
May 8th, 2013

"Hey
There's no rules today.
You steal instead of borrow.
You take all the shapes that I make.
You think
That you think
All the thoughts
That I thought you,
Don't you?
Mutilation's the most
Sincere form of flattery.
If you wanna be me,
Then stand in line like the rest.
Now, do you know what I mean?"

Once again my dreams have proven that there are some things that I cannot let go. Years later, I am still haunted by their ghosts. Maybe it will be a lifelong haunting; a recompense for the hearts I have broken, those that I lost. I do not doubt I deserve it, however without drugs, this is orders of magnitude harder to cope with. Substance is not always the answer, but sometimes it is.

- XV

Sick and Tired... Of Being Sick and Tired
May 13th, 2013

Sleep is a cruel whore, taunting and teasing as the minutes turn to hours, rolling around in bed, frustrated at your inability to accomplish such a simple and necessary task. Bitter? Fuck yes. All the pills in this world cannot seem to remedy my insomnia. It is getting really old now. Well it was getting old three years ago. I am beginning to give up trying. It is pointless to try something again and again, expecting something to change.

My body feels like it is dying. No energy, no drive, nothing. It is just a matter of time before I completely self-destruct.

- XV

The Gathering Storm
May 21st, 2013

Things have been changing recently. I think it is too much for my mind and body to handle. Lately I have become extra miserable, extra insomniac-ish, and all around shittier. I have phases of anger caused by something little, or nothing at all. The lack of sleep is making me delirious and moody. My insomnia has never affected me to this extent. I keep to myself, prefer to be alone, and most of all, I have inevitably fallen back into using drugs. Cocaine has always been an escape to me, however now it seems like the only way to get energy and life into my body. I am not using as heavily as before, but a few MDMA and cocaine fueled nights has spun me out.

This gathering storm is soon to explode. The damage will be unimaginable. Ask me if I care.

- XV

A Failure's Lament
June 5th, 2013

It has been a long time since I last posted. It was not because nothing was going on. Lots has gone on, but I just didn't give enough shits to share it on here, my empty and unread journal. So I speak to no one now, a lament by a failure (maybe not in my eyes).

Temptation has called, and I always answer... Numbing my brain and my body until nothing bothers me anymore. It's not about the thousands of dollars I have put into my addiction (my fix), it's not about my opinion of myself; it's about if people close to me only knew. The thoughts, the drugs, the illness... eating away until all that is left is a silhouette of a person who used to have a future, who used to go to university, who threw it all away for reasons known and unknown. Cleary it seems I do not care. Well that is because I don't. So I take drugs, how is that different than the massive amounts of medications I am on? Sure, legality is the issue, but I do not even care about that. My way of coping may not be 'socially acceptable', but it works for a while, enough to get me by until the next collapse.

My point is that I have chosen how I live, how I cope. Isn't that my choice? Amazing how much it isn't. But I continue to 'live' as I see fit. Some people take the pain head-on and win... Others can't. Like me.

Fuck it. I give up justifying my actions. I'm done.

- XV

Too Far Man, Too Far
June 7th, 2013

That is, if 'too far' even exists for me. I doubt it. No excuses, no explanations, just GTFO if you do not approve.

Feeling different lately. Good, in a way. Bad in another. Maybe it's a phase, maybe it's my evolution.
Sparse details? Yes. Too lazy for explanations and rants.

Live long, and falter.

- XV

Another Life Lost (No God Would Let This Keep Happening)
June 20th, 2013

I was saddened and shocked to hear of another suicide among the small community that was my high school. It always hits hard when it was someone you knew, and even harder (for me especially) to hear it was suicide. A beautiful, young girl took her own life this past Monday. We have already suffered the loss of more friends than I thought would ever happen this early in life. If God exists, he is one sick mother fucker.

I know what it is like to long for Death, to feel like killing yourself is the only way out of the pain and misery. Sometimes I still feel that way. In another way, I wish it was me, not them. Me, not Her. Not Her. But this is a fact of life, unfortunately. A sad reminder that we are not invincible, that loss is a very real, and ever-lingering presence.

Once again, we prepare for another funeral, far too soon. To send another lost life to the other side, whatever it may be.

As I said, I wish it could have been me. It still can be. Maybe it will end at me. Maybe, but not likely. I find it impossible to believe in a loving God that would watch this happen so fucking often and do nothing. NOTHING. All-powerful my ass. He is a dick. An 'omnipotent' DICK. Fuck you.

It should have been me.

- XV

Only the Good Die Young (That's Why I'll Live Forever)
June 20th, 2013

My life has been anything but normal. I would truly hate that, to be honest. The damage I have done to my body is clear in the scars that line my arms and chest. Now when people see me they see scars, telltale of the pain I have been through, as well as the pain I have inflicted upon myself. Despite what people may think (as ignorant as they are), I do not try to hide who I am with long sleeve shirts. Sometimes I believe that the scars are meant to show, even warn, others that I am as ugly on the outside as I am on the inside. My point is that I have made my life about pain. Psychological and physical. A life taken for granted. Despite my hospitalizations, I have continued to damage myself, whether something as simple as a cigarette, or an outright attack in the form of overdose.

Recent events, as stipulated in the last post, have really made me think. Even someone as beautiful as her can feel an ugliness so deep that others are completely oblivious to its existence. Even someone as beautiful as her can be too far gone to save. She succeeded in what I have failed in several times before. I wonder if I had succeeded, if things would be different, even in some small way, to those who had known me. Would she be as affected by my death as I am by hers? Maybe not. Maybe I am susceptible to other people's pain, in that I personalize things. Make them matter to me more than they should.

Regardless, mortality has always been a major theme in my life. As I watch people I know, people from my school, or even family seeming to drop like flies, I wonder why them? Why not me? Why? The answer likely doesn't exist. The Universe, in all its randomness, could possibly have no meaning for these lives lost. On the other hand, the losses can be a straight-forward reminder that life is not something to be toyed with. I have never believed that life is sacred, or a gift, or even laid out before us. We all have equal chances of being doctors, of being drug addicts, or of feeling so helpless that we have no choice but to end our lives, and with it the unrelenting pain that drove us to such a dark place. Just as likely, maybe that place is not so dark. Maybe by ending her life, she truly has found peace. Who is to say that she should have lived, and fought, for something that is potentially unattainable for her?

That is where it really hits home. Was I meant to survive when I nearly bled to death? or when I took enough pills to kill my liver? Maybe, and just as much, maybe not. Maybe I am worse off having survived, whether I know that or not. Maybe I am better off, and am just too stubborn to accept it.

Either way, there is no way to rationalize, explain, or even understand death. No matter what form of death it may be. All I can really say is that I truly hope she is at peace. It is a fight I can understand and sympathize with. RIP, you will be missed by all.

- XV

The Devil Has a Point
June 26th, 2013

Why is it that all the things that are considered 'wrong', always the most fun? Sex, drugs, rock and roll... All things the Church has associated with the Devil. I would rather a night of debauchery than a night spent getting closer to a 'God' that does not exist. One, who even if he did exist, would be quite a douche bag for not stepping in as we aim towards our destruction. I have always asked one question, one that (at least for me) seems to derail everything we are taught to believe:

Why would the Devil punish those who go against God, those who commit 'sin', those who live by sex and drugs, metal music and recklessness?

Aren't those who go against God therefore going WITH the Devil? Wouldn't the Devil greet these people with open arms? That's just my opinion. It's logical. It's how I expect to be greeted when my time comes and I am standing at the Gates of Hell.

Maybe I am just pissed. Maybe that is why I refuse to believe in a loving God. If he is real, that fucker needs to step up. Letting people die that deserve life, allowing pain to run rampant through the world. God is an absentee landlord. Like I said, maybe I'm just bitter, but the way things are leave a bad taste in my mouth. Friends lost, and no answers, no logic. I have dealt with enough pain in my life to know that there is NO ONE looking down on me. NO ONE. Period. It's that simple. However, this world has proven that there is Evil, and therefore a Devil. I expect to be greeted well by him.

Where is God? Nowhere. He left long ago, and I do not blame him. As for my time, it feels as though it is lingering over me, unrelenting, promising me that the pain will end. In time.

- XV

Still Losing
June 30th, 2013

This weekend my Dark Passenger came out again en force. I don't let Him take control as much as I used to, but when I do, it's a fucking shit-show. I put myself into a booze and coke addled haze. Be realistic, did you honestly think I would change that much? I accept who I am, my addictions, my urges, my blatant disregard for my safety... But I also accept the few changes I have made to lessen the aforementioned vices. I feel more in control, but that doesn't mean I always am in control. I am still human (despite how I feel), so of course sometimes I fall victim to this addiction.

She was in my dreams again last night, haunting, tormenting... Years gone by but still I fall victim to her. I'm weak, really, more than I'd like to admit. However, I cannot control where my mind goes as I am asleep. I can't seem to control how that affects me, either. I am guessing that this will not change as much as I would like it to. The past has seemed to have the same vice-grip on my balls as it has for a long time. Clearly I need to let go. Clearly I can't. Poor me.

- XV

Get Off My Fucking Back!
July 2nd, 2013

Advice my mother should realllly take. I'm 23 but still not immune to her incessant nagging. 'Go back to school! Get a job!' I was in school, I DID have a job (several since I was 13)... Did you maybe consider that this lack of motivation might have something to do with the crippling mental illnesses I have? You really think I like where I am right now? That I wouldn't rather be in school, making something of myself?

Well fuck all those doctors who said life wouldn't be easy with my diagnosis. They must be wrong. It isn't a switch I can flick at the drop of a dime. Even the simplest tasks can be hell for me. When I get mad because she keeps pushing the issue, I am the asshole. I am the fucking grumpy prick who is doing nothing with his life. Fuck me for being the way I am. Fuck me, indeed. I'm fucking SICK of people telling me what I should do, how I should feel, and how I should think. Fuck off, leave me alone, and let me deal with my issues. I'm 23 for fuck sakes, it's not like time is running out! Or maybe it is, what the fuck do I know?

- X-fuckin-V

Era: Fall and Depress
July 2nd, 2013

I feel as if I am moving into a new era in my life. I feel changes in my mind and body. May not be changes for the better, but I have a feeling that this will not be something you wanna miss. Fuck shit up, that's what I say.

- XV

Derailed
July 8th, 2013

I wake up in the morning. Empty cocaine baggies, cough syrup, codeine pills, and beer bottles litter the floor. I'm groggy, no memory of the night before. Just random flashes. My chest is covered in dried blood. So is my arm. The ringing in my head is deafening. Is this real? Did I do this? Look left, naked girl beside me. None of these things are triggering my memory.

What happened? How did it get this bad? Will it get worse?

Probably, yes. I deserve it.

- XV

My Own Brompton Cocktail Blend
July 9th, 2013

White, green, salvia, DXM, alcohol, cigarettes, and codeine pills.

Anything I could take to feel a rush that is getting harder and harder to achieve. My relentless march towards destruction is taking its tool. My body is weak and sick, my joints grind, bone on bone, my stomach churns, and my brain nags and nags for more substance. I can't honestly say I know my limit, but I can say any time now, I will reach it, and pass it.

I feel useless without these things in my body. It's hard to wake up, hard to have purpose, and especially motivation.

I have merged with my Dark Passenger. Little light is left, darkness slithers in like a putrid snake. I'll show you how much I can break, how hopeless it is to try to lock me up.

I am Jack's inner monster. He wants out

- XV

Up Shit Creek Without A Paddle
July 10th, 2013

That's a long-winded way of saying things, including me, are fucked. I spend my days looking for uppers, energy, drugs... Then I spend my night swallowing sleeping pills in hopes that I will get even a couple hours of sleep. This cycle is breaking me down. Even more so than most of the shit I do to myself.

Cut again for the first time in several months. Of course I was all fucked on coke, DXM, and codeine pills, I really do not remember it happening. That seems to be a theme in my life... Amnesia.

Whatever you call it, it is a powerful force that pulls and tears at me in every direction. The high is almost never enough, until it is and you freak. You don't know what's going on. To me, that is an adrenaline rush.

Took a handful of sleepers,,. wish me luck in my pointless attempt to sleep.

- XV

Blame Me? Lawl, No... Blame Yourself
July 12th, 2013

*"Take your hatred out on me,
make your victim my head."*

I thought that little nugget from Manson's 'Tourniquet' was appropriate for this post.

FUCK me right? Make me your scapegoat, make me the reason, make it my fault. All while you roll up into a little pity-inducing ball of shit. Wanna blame me? FUCKING BLAME ME!! LET'S SEE YOU GET FUCKING ANGRY!

The problem is, however, that I am not to blame. You made your own choices, said your own words, and dug your own refuse pit. Don't give me any fucking lines about the psych ward. Bitch, I have called that place home over 6 times! I have scars COVERING my arms, medical charts showing I gave myself lead poisoning, that I took 100 Codeine pills just to escape from this Hell!

Thank your lucky fucking stars you aren't like me. Abused, ravaged, dragged through the mud, and tossed away like a used sanitary pad. I have gotten so close to Death that I have stared Him in the fucking eyes and begged him to take me. As a cruel joke, He won't.
The point? Your pity party is leaving, no one bought tickets. All you have is yourself, blubbering like a fucking coward in a room with no

sharp objects.

Next time, FACE me whore.

- XV

Time for Some Fucking Change
July 12th, 2013

Let this unofficial blog declare that there are changes coming. No more will I be a victim of circumstance and depression. I will make those my bitch. Pity is out the fucking window. Drugs... I like drugs, get the fuck over it. People who bitch and whine and do nothing shall be swiftly and, with maliciousness, back-handed.
To the point. I have the choice to let this sickness beat me down, but I also have the choice to accept this sickness and become something more, something better. Cocaingels and bloodsuckers will rise, I will finally be ME... FUCKING ME!
I wasn't built for a normal life. I was brought here to fuck shit up, and fuck it up I shall.

5
4
3
2
1

- XV

Up I Go
July 13th, 2013

With a strong dose of DXM beginning to take effect, I would just like to say that I feel clearer and clearer as the drugs kick in. Nothing matters, no one matters, all that matters is the high. The wonderful, euphoric, hallucinogenic high.

Drugs can tell you a lot about yourself. All you have to do is take them and listen. What do you hear?

tick-tock *tick-tock* *tick---*

- XV

I Can't Write On This Shit
July 13th, 2013

but I can think.... about a lot of things. Will anything STICK??

- XV

And Then There Was Some(thing Weird)
July 16th, 2013

I dislike giving and never receiving (not a sex pun, grow up). Making an effort to share what little I do have with the few I care about. It doesn't always come full circle, however. I am usually pretty protective about how much I 'stick my neck out', as they say. Usually the guillotine comes flying down and my head ends up in a basket.

Anyway, I haven't been myself lately, which sounds weird. I really don't know what "myself" is, but I feel off. Spending most of the day and night in bed, popping benzos and other various downers and mood shifters. It is a funk I would like to be out of soon. I see the doctor Thursday, so maybe he can shed some light on what the Hell is going on with me. TBH it's unnerving. And maybe dangerous... eventually.

- XV

Small Changes
July 19th, 2013

Currently I have nothing that I would like to trash; no comment of depression or loss. That will surely come soon. But for now I ride the high that I have been working on all night. Good feelings rarely happen, so gotta embrace this.

High as FUCK

- XV

The Return to Reality
July 19th, 2013

As thunder rumbles in the background and lightning strikes across the sky, I make a realization - the lifestyle I want (high and free) isn't so easy to accomplish. Now that security has been tightened, the carefree few weeks I have just enjoyed are gone. Of course I will find a way, I always do. I just hate my reality.

My doctor fucks with my meds and I fuck with drugs. My body grows tired of the constant blitzkrieg, but I don't care.

- XV

Dependence (And Visions of Her)
July 21st, 2013

For all the drugs I abuse, it's rare that I focus on one. Lately, (besides cocaine) it has been good old Clonazepam. An incredibly high dose, of course. About 14 mg a day. The recommended dose is less than 2 mg a day. I have been swallowing them like candy, and they have been showing their ugly side effects. Besides the tinnitus (ringing in the ears), I have been less than a Zombie. No concept of time, no emotion, no care in the world. Remember this Clonazepam is being taken with 4 OTHER psychiatric drugs. A cocktail that would put most in a coma.

I don't really know when I am hallucinating, but one person seems to keep showing up.. Her, the one that ruined my life. The one I have tried so fucking hard to hate. I just wanna be numb and forget everything, including her.

- XV

Blood on My Hands
July 22nd, 2013

Looking back on my life, I realize that I have a lot of blood on my hands. Some is mine, some of the girls' whose hearts I ripped out, and some, I do not know how it got there. Self-mutilation used to be a ritual for me, a way to feel pain, to make sure I was still alive, still human. Now my abuse revolves around drugs. Killing myself from the inside is my new 'mission'. I don't care if I die tomorrow, I've lived enough in the past 23 years (at least for me). Others would disagree, but I wouldn't give a shit. This misery is wearing me down, turning me into some sort of demon.

Run motherfuckers, the smile isn't real.

- XV

Worthless
July 22nd, 2013

I know it's not just in my head, but I feel hopeless. I feel discarded. I feel empty. All the drugs I have access to cannot close the gaping hole that has been getting bigger every day. I feel it is safe to say that I do not have one real friend. No one who is there for me, no one who cares.

So I throw up my middle finger in rage and scream FUCK YOU! to all those who have left me over the last few years. Fuck you, get fucked, and fuck off. I am DONE trying to be friendly. I am sick of this mask. Fuck that too. The mask is destroyed.

This isn't all my fault, motherfuckers. YOU did this too. No one is innocent.

- XV

<u>**Alone**</u>
July 22nd, 2013

You can probably tell my posting 3 times in one day, that I cannot make sense of my life. I've used many words to describe it, but the only one that seems to fit is 'empty'.

I am devoid of someone to love, of friends, of motivation, of energy, and of the will to get up and move on. I feel a hole in my chest that keeps getting bigger, spilling everything I have out as it grows.

Instead, day after day, I sit alone... isolated. No one to visit, not even anyone to call or text. This is getting really FUCKING old. What is it about me that seems to repel people? Do I give off a scent of negativity, prompting everyone to run? Fast. Away. It's probably better off that way. It is, however, eating away at what little I have left. I gave everything I had to two certain people, and they took it all and crushed it into a million pieces. I know for a fact that I am not even close to getting over that.

I am pretty certain that no one will read these words, let alone understand what I am going through. My body is physically weakening, as is my mind. I feel that if this goes on any longer, I will finally crumble. Finally do what I should have done years ago. End it, end the misery. No one fucking cares anyways. At my funeral, they will pretend to care, but it's all just a fucking mask.

I am DONE wearing mine. I am going to face these monsters head-on. I really do not care if I lose.

- XV

Exponential
July 23rd, 2013

Don't you just love when the fucking internet crashes right after typing a long post? No draft was made. FUCK FUCK FUCK. My patience, well for everything, is pretty much gone. I drug myself with sleepers all day because I have nothing better to do. My Doctor better come up with something quick. These thoughts are turning into visions of revenge, of hate, of self-destruction, and other things I dare not say on here. Not that anyone reads it. BUT I have been fucked by a few posts years ago.
I just hate where I am. My misery is growing exponentially. I am SO over this fucking bullshit. No friends, no one to vent to except this collection of pixels.

Someday I am going to snap. I'll bring this fucking world down.

- XV

I Fucking Give Up
July 23rd, 2013

Trying often leads to failure, more so in my case. Nothing is ever good enough for my parents. Lately it's been that I am acting like a Zombie. Perhaps it's the massive doses of downers I keep adding to my body.

But NO ONE needs to know, let alone meddle in my affairs. If I wanna be a lifeless waste, then that is exactly what I would be. Same goes for anything. I am 23! Let me make my own choices.
I am just incredibly pissed right now and I am fucking sick of people interfering. As long as the doctor keeps giving me meds, I'm golden.

Fuck you, all of you.

- XV

Dr. Dickhead, MD
July 24th, 2013

I am seeing my doctor once again today. I need blood tests to see if my medications have screwed anything up, which they probably have. I am so fucking tired all the time, no energy to even walk down the street. My body feels like it's slowly dying.

I will also go out on a limb and ask him for Concerta. I think it will help with my fatigue, concentration, and help me focus more. Despite all these benefits, I am afraid he will say no. As you know, I am at my wit's end. SO close to giving up trying to feel better. I am short-tempered, forgetful, and have no focus.

What would be the problem with a weeklong trial, just to see if it makes a difference? I am afraid if it doesn't work. I cannot handle much more of this shit. Next time, I will not fail. That's a promise.

- XV

Psycho or Psychic?
July 24th, 2013

I knew the fucking doctor would do nothing. Except a blood test... Whew, slow down Dr. Dickweed. He told me a specialist would have to prescribe me the Concerta, or something like it. If you know anything about the Canadian health-care system, you know how fucking long it takes to see a specialist of any sort. By then, I'll have completely snapped. I cannot do this much longer. I just can't.

It drives me fucking insane trying to get help from doctors. Listen to me, then write a prescription. SIMPLE.

Or not? They throw all these sleepers at me and wonder why I cannot function during the day. Good thing you went to med school, you fucking quack.

Too tired to ramble on more.

- XV

Born Villain
July 29th, 2013

As I look back on everything I've done, I wonder if I was born this way, or if the world I grew up in made me the way I am. Both make sense, but I think 'evil' is in many ways innate. This world can certainly shape you into a bad motherfucker. I doubt there is a gene for 'evil', but there must be something that one day clicks, a switch in your brain that says, "Fuck you, fuck everyone, fuck this, and fuck everything". Mine seems to have been triggered early on in life, and so I wonder, is this just going to get worse? Will I someday be no longer satisfied with everything I fuck around with. It is fitting that I have 'borderline personality disorder'. As named, most of the time I feel if one more fucking thing goes wrong, my name will be synonymous with Gacy. Then the odd time something inside my head wonders what the fuck I am doing. Why do I need to fuck shit up? Everything I do seems ridiculous. I guess that's what they call a 'conscience' kicking in. But those feelings are inevitably smashed down by the 'evil me'.

I don't know, I just have more fun doing things I am not supposed to than anything else. It's who I am. Stop trying to fucking change me, motherfucker.

Questions are suddenly answering themselves.

- XV

In That Kinda Mood
July 30th, 2013

The one you cannot describe. I feel like something horrible is coming. My heart is in a twist, no, not from the usual substance reason. Something is very wrong, and I do not know what it is. I am not one to worry, especially about the future, let alone my own well-being, but this feeling... it's overtaking me.

I'll let you know when the bomb drops, whatever it may be.

- XV

Vroom Vroom......... CRASH
August 2nd, 2013

My mind is so unclear right now. I blame my four day binge. I feel energetic but tired, wired but relaxed. I actually, all in all, feel good! Good and numb.
But not as numb as it used to make me, sadly. I tend to overthink when on the soft. Things I should not dwell on. People I should not think about.

I guess my point is something has to change. More when sober.

- XV

Oliver Twisted
August 3rd, 2013

Please sir, can I snort some more?

Unreality claws at my brain, trying to take control.... Maybe I'll let them.

- XV

Calling All Skeletons
August 4th, 2013

I have been mentally digging the skeletons out of my proverbial closet. Clearing away the cobwebs, find long lost memories hidden deep inside. The problem is that I am not as ready as I thought I was to face myself. Visions of blood... So much blood. Visions of the snowy forest that one fateful night. Of those I once held, those I once promised everything but gave nothing. Of the psych ward, dark, depressing... trapped. Of all those I've lost in each battle, part of a war with myself. Nothing civil about it.

I swing back and forth between emotions, like bi-polar on hyper-speed. I guess that's what I get with BPD, a condition I have not yet learned to live with. One day will be good, light, and can almost make me forget my misery. The next I will cocoon myself in my sheets, hiding from the world, hating myself and everything around me. The next (like right now) I will feel so utterly depressed and hopeless that it almost chokes me to death. I wish there was a cure. Medication after medication has sent my body haywire. I feel I am too far gone by now. Actually I know I am too far gone to save. Physically, my body is tired and weak, and my brain chemistry would likely frighten any neurobiologist. Mentally, as you can obviously tell, I am a fucking wreck. My mind is cluttered and broken, beyond repair.

I am too far gone to save now. Jump ship and swim like Hell. The ride is going to get bumpier yet, I promise you.

- XV

Is This What You Wanted?!?!
August 4th, 2013

Are you motherfuckers happy? Are you proud of what you have done? All you fake motherfuckers, hiding behind some mask because you are frightened of just how UGLY you really fucking are. Call me the freak? Call me fucked up because I am mentally ill? Your ignorance will certainly be your downfall, if I don't get to you first.

Fakes. Liars. Back-stabbers. Self-righteous assholes. Get off your fucking high horse before I pull you down, cut you open and show you what your heart looks like before you die.

(CLEARLY this is anger talking. This is in no way a threat to a specific person or group, so settle the FUCK down and if you don't like it, DON'T READ IT!)

I am fucking angry beyond anything I have felt before. So depressed that 'depression' seems like a big step up.

One final message to you scum. Filthy molesters. Egotistical scum bags... Enjoy your fake high life now, because I promise you, it will come crashing down, and when it does, I will have the last laugh.

- XV

Losing All Control
August 8th, 2013

My emotions are escaping me. They are becoming more numb and dull. I don't have much control over anything anymore, as if my body is on auto-pilot.... Headed for a mountain.

- XV

Friends Are For The... Uhh... Not Me
August 8th, 2013

I ask myself why I even have a Facebook? The few friends I do have don't talk to me, all I do is creep. Like a pathetic loner in a dark room, wishing he was different... *Looks around*

My friends have dropped like flies. The loyal ones that have told me "I'll be there for you, no matter what."... I wish I could rape them with their own lies. Friends I lived with, cared about.... TRUSTED. Gone. All fucking gone.
What made me so fucking disposable? Now, I do it intentionally. Don't get close or I WILL hurt you. I will ruin your fucking life.

- XV

A Positive Note
August 9th, 2013

My brother is coming back home soon, very briefly on his way to Edmonton for the military. I haven't seen him since Christmas and that is just too fucking long.

I really, really need this. Things are not going well.

- XV

Psychopathy Dawning
August 9th, 2013

I should be scared. I should be worried. But I am not. The visions in my head, the thoughts, the obsessions, and the fantasies all dance a macabre number as if my head was their stage. Things that once scared me no longer do. All I fear now is what I know I could become. It is a long way from thoughts to actions, but I feel that I am on the road to action. Maybe. I do not know for sure. Maybe it's just a twisted phase in the life of a lonely druggie with no friends and no escape (well..)

I am just losing my mind, my sense of self, my sense of reality, and my sense of right and wrong. Are these things that could even be recovered? Or will a smouldering black-box be the only explanation of what happened to me? Four written journals, and this online journal that no one knows about (except one) sum up my life.

- XV

The Fuse Gets Ever Shorter
August 9th, 2013

An hour and a half with my mother is enough to drive me to inject bleach into my arm. It's like she is working with half a brain. Fucking plain stupid. Fucking STUPID. She makes me want to snap. My temper is getting tested every day and soon, I know I will fucking snap. She is my mother, but holy shit how did I come from that?

Maybe it's just my own short fuse, for everything, not just her. I feel a rage so raw and building that I am frantically searching for a way to get rid of it without a body count.

NB. I love my mother regardless.

A friend just surprised me with a powdery treat. Lookin' up.

- XV

No Escape
August 10th, 2013

I have created a prison for myself. A dark hole with barbed wire surrounding both the inside and the outside (well I don't mind a few more scars). Keeping people out, and keeping myself locked in. These four walls are closing in. I claw at the dirt and filth around me, but it doesn't do any good. There is no escape from this Hell. That was by design. Eventually I will have to face the fact that there is no winning. No getting better, no one out there for me, no point in pressing on. My half-assed approach to life has been the only sign of my attempts to fix what's wrong.

The problem is I am too deep. There is really only one escape, one true way out of this. One very, very taboo and 'unimaginable' way out. Maybe I should just commit myself. Might be for the greater good of the world.

Nothing but that will end the depression, the pain, the loneliness, the self-destruction... Fuck even the mountains of debt piling up on me. The selfish, painful end I long for is so fucking selfish, but that reason is becoming not enough to keep the thoughts away. I don't know what's after Death. Maybe it's worse than this, and I deserve it. Maybe it's better. Maybe it's nothing. Whatever it may be, it is seeming more and more like the only decision I have.

My days are numbered.

- XV

Words
August 10th, 2013

I am writing a lengthy summation of what is included in this journal, plus some bonus material to sweeten things up. Not as easy as I thought. Will keep updates.
- XV

Second Class Citizen
August 13th, 2013

I am so fucking sick and tired of being treated like shit. If I say something, I'm being a smart-ass, if she says it, it's perfectly fucking A-OK. Well fuck that. That is not how shit works, I don't care who you are. You drove me to cut for the first time in over a year, CONGRATS!!

Only you can pull off such a fucking feat. All I do is the slave work, fuck anything else, right? Well we will see. I will show you exactly how fucking bad I can be. How fucking psychotic, how sarcastic, how difficult, how fucking 'delightful'. Watch your fucking back. The fuse has been lit.

- XV

Reconcile This
August 15th, 2013

First, before I get into my angry ramblings, I was able to get my tattoo fixed... professionally. I fucking love it, worth every penny.

Now onto other matters. I came home to see that someone I had all but cut from my life was there. First, I was filled with anger. Of course this made me look like an asshole so I had to play nice. I am not even allowed to be still want someone out of my life? I don't care if they are all broken up and going to rehab... No longer my fucking business. Eventually I donned the happy mask (I never like folding like that). But I was proud of how long I stood my ground, and even still, I do not just forgive and forget so fucking easily. Don't fool yourself. You did this, not me.

I fucking hate being forced to face things I have let go of already. My passive-aggressive nature has allowed me to face things at a comfortable distance while still getting my point across.

My extra-long write up should be completed soon. Stay tuned.

- XV

Crystal Castles
August 15th, 2013

It's amazing what a little R**i****i* (intentionally masked) can do when you're having a shit night. The *** in it makes for a fantastical night, but maybe I am over-selling it.

Crystal Castles grooves in the background as I type this. Why would I want a normal life? There, answered a question from a while ago.

I straight up shouldn't type on here right now.

- XV

I Own the Night
August 16th, 2013

I thrive in darkness. The night seems more peaceful, a time I can be more free. It suits me, but not in that "I'm so emo" way.

Tonight is a new night.

Watched Natural Born Killers today... Love that movie.

- XV

I Am Jack's Bleeding Heart
August 17th, 2013

It seems I leave a lot of heartbreak and despair in my wake. I don't do it intentionally, it's just my condition (as a fallible, screwed up human being). Except I do not feel human sometimes. Someone who causes this much pain surely must be something else, something worse. I look for proof and it is easily found. All the friends and girlfriends I had once loved and held are now absent, most with a painful separation in their memories. I feel like when someone gets close to me, it is like they are pulling a pin on a grenade with an unknown fuse. It will blow up, but the question is when. Can I keep letting people pull the pin? Will I ever stop exploding? Will someday someone pull the pin and nothing happens?

A look at my history makes that notion laughable. I am damaged, hemorrhaging life on the inside and out. I sometimes think they key is finding someone as damaged as I am (which is a Herculean task). Maybe two damaged individuals will make a better situation, as in mathematics, where two negatives multiply into a positive. 'Maybe' is all I have. 'What ifs' get you nowhere but worse off because you know that what you dream will never happen. It is a losing battle of fantasy and harsh, violent reality.

I gave my heart to someone already. They stomped on it. I got a second chance and they broke it into pieces. How can I give someone the shattered remnants of a heart that belong(s)/(ed) to someone else? It's Humpty Dumpty all over again. Sorry Kings men, sorry Horses. This one is a lost cause. Get the dust pan and throw it in the trash.

- XV

An Essay-Like Clarification Of Me
August 17th, 2013

Preface

I have written dozens upon dozens of entries. My mood goes up, down, and sideways. My mindset changes in a flash. My view of others and the past are always in flux. Most of all, my idea of my self is never concrete, nor shall I expect it to be. Here, I will try to summarize months of ups and downs, years of abuse; a vast amount of yes, no, and maybe so. For all about to read, good luck. It is not my aim to please or mince words. Read with caution, and realize when metaphor is metaphor. So we begin.

Part I

Realize, first and foremost, that no person is simple. No person operates in one way, the same way, every time. Some of us operate in more ways than can be numbered. People are funny (take the definition as you will) that way. One minute they can be smiling, happy, and calm... The next, they could be angry and inconsolable. You surely get my point.

That being said, personally I have yet to find a category in which I fit. Categories are inaccurate but necessary ways of understanding types of people. Maybe my category is just that, I don't have one. I wander like a soul with no eyes, looking for my place, but finding nothing. Eternal nothingness. I do not put myself in such high regard as to say I am the only one who wanders from place to place looking for themselves, but this is my journal and will treat it as such.

I hope my words will inform and answer, not confuse and befuddle. This is no death note, no goodbye; just the prose of a man unknown to himself. A stranger to his own shadow. Maybe this is written more for me; written to understand and make sense of an existence full of pain and despair. Now before I begin, there is good in my life, and I accept and appreciate all of it. But this is not what this is about. It's about what really makes a man - pain.

Growing up wasn't a big sob story full of heartache. It was pretty average. So what made me, me?

Part II

I do not want to define myself by a diagnosis, by some mental illness. However, it does sum me up pretty well, to be honest. Borderline Personality Disorder is a complex and misunderstood illness that I will not try to explain here. Search in your time if you are interested in what it is. The symptoms, however, will become apparent as I go on (however long that may be). Realize as well that mental disorder is different for everyone. It would be a huge mistake to call my symptoms 'textbook'.

This part will explain me in summation the best I can. On the outside I am introverted, socially awkward, and nothing girls take a double take at (though not ugly, let me be clear). I am dry and sarcastic, very black and white, and a bona fide smart-ass. I seemed to be smart enough to get into a great university (more on that later), and enjoyed the short time spent there. I used to be outgoing, but since the depression kicked in, I have retreated inside myself.

Now, I am a recluse and a loner. Closed off from all those who betrayed or hurt me. What is 'wrong' with me is all to do with psychological affliction, or something similar, and events in my past I have yet to get through. The only place I can be honest and open is on an online journal no one reads. And here we are.

Note the lack of information about myself. I just don't really know what to say. There isn't much. Read on, find out, I guess.

Part III

How do I act? How do I take on life's little curve-balls? Well that has recently changed. I was such a fucking push over. Take it like a bitch and say nothing. Now, however, fuck with me and you will get it right back. I don't care who you are. I don't care what you can do or who you know. Never back down from ignorant fucks that test you. I am still as passive-aggressive as they come, but the odd time I will snap. I bottle up so much shit it turns into incomprehensible stress and rage. The issue is, I have nothing to take that out on but myself (and the odd time someone else). I don't always act how I want to, or how I say I should. That is the weakness in me. But that is dwindling. Being replaced by a growing urge to massacre. Metaphorically, of course…

Time will tell how I come to act, how I come to react. If this trend continues, things will get ugly. Fast.

Part IV

My world view is, as you can guess, cynical. I hate just about everyone and everything. I think everything is stupid and everyone is ignorant. Except me, who I believe has a clearer understanding of things. Not to sound full of myself as you know I am not…

There are four certainties in this world, four things that each person will face, and these are the most important themes we have:

Love
Hate
Life
Death

These are all interconnected, playing a part in each other's existence. You cannot have love without hate, life without death, love without life, hate without death, etc. Things are black and white. Things are simple. The grey area is for people who cannot decide what they believe, or who have no opinion about anything. Love and death may be the two most important; the most connected. I have learned this the hard way throughout the years. Take these four entities and make your own conclusions, I won't do the thinking for you.

Part V

Drugs are fun. A simple truth. But they are so much more than that, too. Drugs have shown me sides of myself I never imagined. Ideas I never thought possible. Truths that should be simpler to see. Of course, with this much good comes a certain amount of bad. Socially, I am an addict. Fuck those labels. I am who I am, not what you label me as.

My history with drugs is a long and complicated one. I do like how there is a drug for everything. A pill to make you numb, a pill to make you dumb, a powder for some energy, a plant for some relaxation, and a rock for the perfect high. I had always been so scared of the stigma that comes with using drugs. However I have learned, through years of trial and error, to not give a fuck. I like drugs. They like me. Simple.

But of course it isn't all simple. The grey areas are widespread and the drugs themselves seem to have personalities of their own. Just like I believe there is a song for every mood, there is a drug for every mood as well. There is a drug for every problem, for every amount of pain and suffering. For each person and personality.

All I am saying is drugs have a place in the world, and in my past, present, and future. They are a necessary 'evil', they keep me sane.

Part VI

Hopefully this has cleared up some questions you may have had, or at least killed a bit of time before something important. I can barely keep track of my own thoughts and emotions, let alone spell them out for you. All I can say is this: Live long, and falter

New Beginning?
August 21st, 2013

"See a new beginning rise behind the sun
We can't ever catch up to them as fast as we run "
- Running to the Edge of the World, Manson

I have been accepted to College starting January 2014. All that science shit, preparing me for a possible career as a paramedic. Wouldn't that be ironic, with all the ambulance rides I have had in the past few years. Anyway, the optimistic side of me says this is good, I am moving forward, leaving the past behind. The pessimist in me says, "Am I really?" There is always a lot of doubt when pursuing something like this. I'm not really nervous and uneasy, but I am sure that will come in due time, as the new year gets closer.

As for leaving my past behind, I doubt it will be that easy. Almost four years later and she still haunts my dreams. A demon disguised as an angel, giving out pain like fucking Halloween candy. It might be something I never am able to let go of...

- XV

A Pre-Post
August 25th, 2013

There is a lot I need to get off my chest. Today is hard for me, it's her birthday and for yet another year I cannot see her or talk to her. Why this still bothers me is both clear and confusing. Anyway, when I have time later I will elaborate. For now, gotta put on my happy face and get through the day.

The Actual Post
August 25th, 2013

I want to start off by saying: FUCCCCKKKKKKK!!!!!!

Ahh, much better. Now, I pretty much covered it in my earlier post. I am fucking depressed today. It's her birthday. Therefore it is time to get away from this world for the night. Time to forget all the bullshit and things that are pissing me off. Yes, this is another DXM night. Let the forgetful-out of body-wooshy experience begin!

Off I go, into a world I control. Where they haven't left. Where I feel no pain, no heartache. Wish I could stay here.

- XV

Slo-Mo-Tion
August 27th, 2013

Now that I have finally applied to college, everything seems to be going so fast. Too fast for someone used to living in slo-mo-tion. I still have 3 months to prepare, but I guess the idea of such a big change, a real start on a future, scares the shit out of me. I am used to being myself, with the depression and all my drama, it will be hard to make such a big change. I will try like Hell to avoid faking it. Maybe this is the start all of this bullshit has led up to. Maybe I have done my time and finally have the chance to move forward.

Or it could all go horribly wrong, but I am pushing that thought out of my head right now. While negativity has served me well up until now, I will have to change a lot about me and my attitude before I could ever dream of succeeding in this whole college endeavor. Point is, I already finding myself panicking. That's just my style. I know I can kick college's ass. Bring it.

- XV

Down The Rabbit Hole
September 2nd, 2013

I have once again gone too far. A new drug, a new addiction, and cravings that leave me hurting for more. I told myself this was over, but a new acquaintance has shown me that the very drug I said was nothing too great, can be. Money is hemorrhaging out of my account and I once again find myself between a 'rock' and a hard place (so to speak). In a big way, I don't care. The feeling that nothing else matters, the relaxation, the heart-pumping energy, and the euphoria all make it worthwhile. Though I am on my track to college, I know that I will not let this stop me from getting there. Sometimes, I just lose control and fall down the rabbit hole... Into a dream world that is my very own.

- XV

So Screwed
September 7th, 2013

My new 'hobby' has left me broke, not even a week into the month. I am so screwed that I have no idea what to do, let alone how to get out of this grave I have dug for myself. Will I have to admit the truth? Can I scrape by without anyone knowing? Or is this the inevitable fall, just when I am getting my life together. For once, I am truly scared of the future... Specifically the near future. I am trapped. Pinned down, once again, by my addictions. If the truth gets to be known, I am FUCKED. There is no other outcome than that. I put myself here, I'll deal with it... But Jesus Tittyfucking Christ this is going to be one long, hellish ride.

I may not make it out of this. I may lose my home, school, family... everything. Maybe I deserve this. Maybe I am destined to be this guy... this low... this much of a failure. This stuff grabbed me by the balls and took everything. If this all comes crashing down, there may not be a chance, or even a reason, to restart. This might just be my true end. Then I will no longer cause pain, heartache, or be a failure. I will just be gone. Away from it all. I wonder what circle of Dante's Hell is reserved for people like me. Whatever it is, I deserve it.

- XV

The Low End of Low
September 9th, 2013

Due to my situation, I have to figure out a plan that doesn't leave me homeless, in jail, or dead by my own hand. Right now those seem like the only three options. Everything else would be a miracle. Suicide has been in the back of my mind for years. Everyone has a different outlook on it, but I see it as a viable way to end the pain and misery of life. I am up to my balls in debt, have about a dollar to my name, just fucked up again with drugs... People have ended their lives for less. I am out of options. If my family finds out I fucked up AGAIN, I may as well be dead.

I'm not here to argue right or wrong, or any philosophy considering live vs. death. I am stating bone-hard fact. I am fucked and there is very little I can do to prevent catastrophe. I have accepted long ago that I will die early in life. It was just a matter of what would set me off...

BOOM.

- XV

Really? Just, Really?
September 10th, 2013

Do you think that I am that FUCKING stupid? You got me into this shit and as we (I) try to clean up, you keep making "runs" for other people, knowing full-well there is something in it for you. But why fucking lie to me? I am not oblivious to the behaviour of an addict. You are going over to that place. And you think I don't realize? Well fuck me. I do not care about the drugs, I care about the principle. I have covered a lot of ass for her, now she treats me like Helen-FUCKING-Keller, deaf, dumb, and blind.

Whatever, fuck it right? I am only trying to get away from this shit and you fucking TRIGGER me. Well done there, doctor.

- XV

PS. A very special thank you to an amazing friend. What has been the only light in these dark days? Without you I would be nothing. I hope you know how I fell and how much you have saved my life.

Cornered
September 11th, 2013

I feel cornered. By the sudden expectations for school, for work, and for sobriety. Under pressure I turn into a hand-grenade, fuse half pulled. My anxiety and stress disorders do not help this either. I think I know what the best path is, but can I follow it? It seems steep and unending.

Then I look down. Dante's version of Hell lies beneath my feet. I belong to so many circles of Hell that I must have to be torn into pieces, each receiving a punishment fit for my crimes. Bodies writing in agony, laying bloody in their own shit. Serpents biting and hissing. Each circle further has a worse horror waiting for the sinner. I don't necessarily believe this to be true, but fuck... Makes you think. Dante was forever scarred by the horrors he saw. He sent a very clear message.

I wrote "Sometimes the best or only option is the one that causes us to recoil in horror." I can be argued on that, but it is a clear point. The exit isn't always simple as a door. The right thing to do in a given situation may be horrific, but necessary.

As for me? I have no choice but to watch as my world twists and turns around me, waiting for that possible explosion, where I will not make it out alive.

-XV

It's That Time of The Month
September 12th, 2013

....When I have to see my psychiatrist. I am so close to my breaking point with everything going on that if he ignores me I will fucking snap. I cannot handle this stress, this pain, this depression... It's killing me. I can spend an hour counting the ways I am in pain, but this isn't a My Chemical Romance album. All I know is that I am at the end of my rope and I am more than willing to let go if need be. Load me up with pharmaceuticals, IDGAF! Make the fucking pain GO AWAY. Let me sleep, let me smile for once without faking it, let me get out of this Hell and move on. Oh and make it so I don't feel like ripping everyone's throat out every day.

But you won't. You'll tell me I need to get a hobby. Say that today doctor... I DARE you.

- XV

Change The Dose... That'll Do It
September 12th, 2013

I like when my cynicism is proven when I sit in that chair and the doctor fucks me over. Due to my increased depression, anger, and anxiety, he has decided to once AGAIN increase the dose of a dangerous drug. One that makes me a zombie, one that makes me hallucinate.

Well fine FUCKER. Let's do it your way. You are playing my game, bitch, and you will not win.

- XV

Nothing Is Ever Free
September 12th, 2013

She isn't in the door 10 seconds and already I got yelled at. She asks me a question then keeps talking. I ask if I can answer... Her reply? "DON'T FRIGGIN START WITH ME TONIGHT! NOT AFTER LAST NIGHT!"

Wow... I didn't fucking do anything last night, so what is her problem? Menopause doesn't suit her well, let me say. I do not have to put up with this shit at twenty-fucking-three years old. I want out and I am stuck here. Nowhere to go, no place to run to. No sanctuary. Just me, my demented thoughts, and all the medications I take to 'make everything okay'.

I just don't know what to fucking do anymore. I am screwed. A leper that nobody fucking wants. Strewn out on the muddy ground, pissed and stepped on. I can hear the murmurs of the passers-by, all saying what a failure I am, how pathetic I was. I am barely human. I want to cut to prove I can bleed but I can't bring myself to do it. I have enough fucking scars from the pain I have been through.

FUCK IT FUCK IT FUCK IT FUCK IT!!!

- XV

Pull The Pin... I Fucking Dare You
September 14th, 2013

As I have been writing recently, a lot of anger, hate, rage, and emotion is building up inside me. I have a feeling that all it will take to set me off is one poor soul who either intentionally or accidentally pulls the pin (I am the grenade in this metaphor). I just can't stand being at this point where if pushed, I will fall.

With my mother I feel I cannot say anything without being attacked for it. Yeah, I am sarcastic and an ass sometimes, but then why does she get to yell and I have to lay down and take it like some prison bitch. I am fucking tired of being the prison bitch, but I cannot fight back. Too much is riding on me staying here and going to college in January.

Happy anniversary to one of the greatest records of all time, Mechanical Animals... Gonna be rocking it all day. Seems fitting for my mood anyways.

- XV

One Is Too Many, and A Thousand Would Be Even Better
September 15th, 2013

... A play on the NA saying.

Seems to fit me better this way, I think. Addicts are persistent and cunning, using whatever they can to get their fix. Though not all are bad or do bad things. Some can just manipulate a situation to work in their own favour. Anyway, what I mean is that an addict will always be an addict, even if they haven't used in years. I happen to have several addictions, none all that positive. I know what they are (in my head) and I do not deny them, nor do I see them as flaws.

My point is that I am walking a very dangerous line between success and utter failure. It's getting harder to walk straight and when I fall, I hope I land on the right side, whichever that may be.

- XV

Not All It's Cracked Up To Be
September 17th, 2013

I never thought anything could grab you by the balls so fast and hard that before you know it, everything is a haze. You remember bits and pieces, the money, the feeling, the euphoria... But in the end, I do not find it worthwhile. The emotions and physical bullshit is overwhelming and takes away from the experience. Stuff like this should remain recreational. Once in a while. But it rarely works out that way.
Only time will decide where this takes me. I want it to take me far away. I am not strong enough to fight these demons. I give in too easy. Maybe that is just the way I like it.

- XV

Hurt II
September 18th, 2013

"I hurt myself today
To see if I still feel
I focus on the pain
The only thing that's real
The needle tears a hole
The old familiar sting

Try to kill it all away
But I remember everything"

Despite the insane amount of substance abuse over the last few weeks, I still find the hole in my chest tearing open more and more. I seem to be falling, but I cannot hit the ground. Sometimes I want to. At least I know there is no way I can go lower. Makes sense to me, maybe not you. Rock bottom is far from where I am, as it goes. But emotionally I am closer than I think. All the usual anxiety, depression, pain, regrets, hate, etc. is still there and getting worse. The pin on the grenade trembles now, threatening to pull out like someone fucking without a condom. Something has to change. I keep saying that but nothing ever does, at least in the way you want it to.

- XV

To The Core
September 18th, 2013

For the sake of this post, let's forget the drugs and self-abuse. Let's look at the core. Is it as black as her demon eyes? Is it necrotic and decrepit? Or have I been wrong all along? Only I can come closest to knowing what is inside. My horrific thoughts, my haunting past, my often malevolent attitude towards people in general (more so to a few select individuals), and so on. I do not identify myself this way by choice. I do not feel like this for sympathy or shock value. This is the naked truth, and it scares me to Death sometimes.

Rewind almost 4 years. I can see my breath in the night air. Snow falls lightly from the sky as my gaze is drawn to her. Something's wrong. There's blood... a lot of blood. Did I do this? She was losing consciousness as I stared in horror. I checked my hands... bloody. Everything went numb and as night fades, her sobs echo on and on. In fact, they still do. LET GO! they tell me. Impossible. If they only knew. The blood, the pain, the cold... Fear in its rawest form. The image is certainly branded into my memories. No amount of therapy nor substance can ever make it go away. What have I done? That night set many things into motion. I lost her, months later. She left. The truth is, I lost her on that cold, horrible night where the snow was stained red.

Too much has happened, too much pain and suffering at my hands for me to say anything other than I am blackened to the core. They have a place in the Afterlife for people like me. Full of blood and gore, repeating images of the most haunting night of my life. Where you can never let go, never forget, and never get closure. Sure sounds like where I am now...

- XV

Listen Up XV...
September 19th, 2013

Yes, shit is rough. Rougher than you can handle at most times. But you are pathetic. Unable to let go, unable to move on, to mend yourself. You are so fucking stubborn that you are ruining your own life. YOU push yourself down. Snort that blow, pop those pills, and hit the pipe. Where the fuck did that ever help you? You wanna forget? YOU CAN'T. Life sucks but shit happens. More so to some people. I would call you a coward, but that's not the right word. You are not ignorant to your problems, you just ignore them... And often make them worse.

Let me warn you. If you keep this path going, you will fall. Hard. You think you know pain, rock bottom? I will show you fucking pain. I am your worst enemy. I can push you down barely lifting a finger. I send you mixed messages for a reason. Sometimes you just need to nut the fuck up and face those Demons, but sometimes all you can do is curl up and let life fuck you. I still think you are pathetic, but after everything you have done to yourself and others, it would be hard not to be.

Is there a way out? Yes. But it is not pretty. Is there a way to cope? Yes, and it's better than the easy way out. Just be warned. Someday soon, without warning or even provocation, you will explode. Who will you take with you? Will you even try to avoid it?

I am you. Your worst nightmare. Keep playing Russian Roulette. I'll pull the trigger too.

- (XV)

Nut Up or Shut Up
September 20th, 2013

The last post was right, for the most part. I sit around feeling sorry for myself and do nothing to get better. I just don't see a light at the end of the tunnel. No direction to go where everything will suddenly be okay. I am trapped, you realize. Putting on a brave face is an illusion. Trickery. So then what's the point? There isn't one. I am living on the brink of collapse, ready to fall. Willing to fall. Does that make me weak? Sure, I guess.

I have tried everything to move on, to let go, to get better, but I always end up back in the same shitty spot I started in. Before you lecture me, take a look at yourself. Hell, put yourself in my shoes. You don't know hopelessness. Emptiness. Anyway, that last post was a failure bud. I don't need your fucking fortune cookie bullshit. There is no magic way for me to suddenly snap out of this depression. I agree, someday I may be free of this burden, but until then, it's my cross to bear. I don't want to drag people into my shit anymore. It's the reason everyone is gone in my life.

Fuck you.

- XV

Jobs... Fuck
September 20th, 2013

I went out job searching today. Not my most fruitful endeavor. I was riddled with anxiety as managers asked me questions and put me on the spot. I froze. I choked. Am I trying to get a job because I think I am ready, or because I think I have to, being so poor. I think the latter. Work. Just seems like the thing to do in life. But I still have way too many wounds that have yet to heal, too much I need to (and refuse to) let go of.

I can see it now... A sales job. All I can think of is if they are looking at my hideously scarred arms. I am not quite self-conscious about the scars, but it sure will not be an easy thing to face in the workplace.

Maybe I should just stay on disability until school starts. See how that goes and move on from there. There are just so many expectations of me that I know I will just disappoint.

Need a new post... Gotta vent.

- XV

Venting
September 20th, 2013

FUCK YOU. I am tired of trying to be what everyone wants me to be. Tired of failing. Tired of trying so hard to please and ending up a fucking piece of shit. FUCK YOU!

FUCK FUCK FUCK.

I have so much fucking anger and tension built up, I feel that I will burst. As I have said in my last posts, the pin just needs to be pulled. Someone fucking pull the pin. DO IT. Motherfucker.

I am so goddamn tired of trying to keep up with society's standards. How I should act, how I should feel... Well fuck that. I am pissed off, depressed, and the anxiety is killing me. Why can't they accept ME? Because it's not the 'norm'. FUCK that word. FUCK what it represents. Maybe for me, this is the norm. Who are they to say who I should be? I don't tell anyone how to live so why do I get the fucking lectures.

GET FUCKED!

- XV

Writer's Block
September 20th, 2013

I am feeling like I want to write. Get things off my chest (more than I already do). Except something different. Maybe not so emo and narcissistic. I just can't make a connection to what's in my brain to words I can type out or write down. Maybe it's the clonazepam for I have put myself in. I don't even want to say how much I've taken, even if I could remember. It's not something you can OD on, it just makes you dopey and sleepy. But something is keeping me awake and alert too. A need to express.

Okay, I'll be honest. The clonazepam is meant to try to numb the thoughts in my head, make them go away. They are macabre and disturbing, even to me. I live in fear of writing out what is in my head as it has been used against me. Trust is something I have long since given up on. History repeats itself, and my history fucking blows.

Maybe in an hour or two I can come up with something. Writing about nothing seems ironically pointless.

- XV

I May Be Fucked Up, but I Can Still Feel Something
September 21st, 2013

It never seems to be enough. Living at home at 23 was NEVER my plan, but I have proven that living by myself has disastrous consequences. It's no easy ride here. Chores and responsibilities all fall into my lap. Which I can handle, but often my mother says something that makes me want to boot her in the face. Take today for example. She went out for groceries and came back, acting all weird. I asked what was up and she said (I shit you not): "I am tired of coming home to depression." Well guess what, fucker? I AM SICK OF BEING DEPRESSED! You think I just like the label, or I am role playing? You think I like spending every day alone staring at my meds, wondering if there's enough to kill me?

I am sure as a parent, it is frustrating, but do NOT fucking put this on me. I live it every day, all day. I live with what comes with depression; the insomnia, mood swings, lethargy, no appetite, isolation... You get the point. Live ONE fucking day in my shoes. Guess what... I am sick of her coming home and making me feel worse for having this disease. If she only knew the pain I am really in, what was behind the mask I wear for her, she would shut the fuck up and maybe listen.

I gave up long ago trying to explain how I feel. It falls upon deaf ears anyway. All I want is one day free of this. But I can't. SO I have to deal with it, and SO DOES SHE. Otherwise kick me the fuck out so you can be smug in a depression-free home.

- XV

On A Positive Note
September 22nd, 2013

Hung out with an old friend today. An old best friend who was the drummer in my band(s). It was good to see him after so long. Maybe this is the (re)start of a good, stable friendship. I hope so, I don't think I can take any more rejection. I want to thank him for giving me the chance to show I am not so fucked up (on the outside, as that's all he will see).

- XV

Fuck You Muchly
September 23rd, 2013

"Haters call me bitch
Call me faggot call me Whitey
But I am something that you'll never be"

Made the mistake of messaging an ex today. I thought her and I were on good terms, but fuck was I wrong. I guess her bf got involved and told me to: 'Fuck of fagget'. Now before we address the spelling issues, I have never met this cunt. Why wouldn't my ex just reply and tell me the truth? Why did a slew of name calling and shit have to happen? He called me a 'sick fuck'. Rumors tend to spread like wildfire, but that I'm a sick fuck? If I ever see this cunt in person, I WILL show him just how fucking 'sick' I really am. He thinks he knows me by what others say? He has no fucking idea what I could do to him. This is not a threat, it's just fact.

I will not be judged by some random douche that cannot even spell. This is what I get for innocently asking an ex how school was going. Well FUCK ME for trying to be nice, forget the bullshit of the past. It is clear to me now that the past is never really the past. So I say fuck it, I give up. Her and that cunt really make a great team...

Next time bud, say it to my face. I dare you. I really fucking dare you. I'll show you sick.

- XV

And I Ran...
September 23rd, 2013

Today was fucking rough. Being treated like garbage for asking a simple question. I just wanted to know how she was. The following assault by her bf and then herself left me feeling lower than low. The small amounts of hope I had built crumbled. The trust I had exploded into painful shards, as if to say 'You're an idiot for trusting again'. I am an idiot. Every move I make worsens every aspect of my life.

I feel like an empty shell that people just like kicking around. I'm too weak to do anything about it, even if I wanted to. Her bf told me to 'Pull the trigger already!' Well motherfucker, if I pull the trigger, it will be twice. Once for you, once for me. Don't fucking tempt me, I am warning you. I am not just talking all tough on this journal. If he wants to say that shit about me, I will be his worst fucking nightmare... I will be his fucking executioner.

So with all this tearing and ripping of my being, I ran... Right into the warm welcoming arms of substance. And for a while, I was worlds away. The crash hasn't really been that bad, but I know I am coming back down to the same old shit life I have been complaining about for years. Isn't that always the case?

Well I am hoping tomorrow is a better day. I am sick of this shit. I hope I can even sleep. That seems to be too complicated for my body without the aid of several pharmaceuticals.

- XV

Bad to Good to Bad Again
September 24th, 2013

I woke up feeling shitty, questioning why I should even bother getting out of bed. Every day is the same old shit. Sit around, do nothing and fall deeper into depression. Days like today, where I manage to get some magical substances, however, make it sort of worth it. In the end it totally is not, but all I care about right now is the fix. The quick fix. It's no secret that I do not want to live this life. That I thrive in the abstract world of substance. I try to balance but one side always topples over leaving me down in the shit.

Now, after the substance is gone, I am back to wondering why I even try. Misery follows me everywhere. Bad luck clings to me, and everyone I get close to seems to end up wanting nothing to do with me. It's obvious that the common denominator is me. ME. As in 'it is ME that fucks everything up'.

What do I have to show for the last few years? Hospital visits, overdose, scars that will never heal (inside and out), no friends, no hope, nothing inside, no aspirations for the future... I am a fucking mess. A total fucking mess. Escape seems unlikely. At least, the kind of escape where I come out feeling better. I don't want to be a burden, or this useless, or this fucking miserable. I often wonder if people around me would be better off without me.

Would the one who told me to 'Pull the trigger already' be at my funeral? Will she feel guilt? Regret? Or just sad that someone she knows is dead. Would the one that I cannot get out of my head be there? After almost 4 years of separation? Would many people even turn up?

I have burned a lot of bridges. There aren't many left to cross.

- XV

College
September 25th, 2013

I went to the college today to sort out finances and my disability and shit. Things actually went well, and I am looking forward to starting in January. The only fear I have is of crowds. Crowded lecture halls, group work, line-ups, eyes everywhere, looking and seeing.

I am not worried about the course itself. You know I am not one to boast (as I have little to boast about), but I will stomp this course. I won't get cocky, I will just do what I do best: Get high grades. Then when the time comes for the Paramedic program, I will be a shoe-in.

As for the ex that took an innocent question and turned it into all-out war, I don't blame you. I hate myself, how can I expect others to want to be in my life. But the sudden escalation was uncalled for. Your bf showed extreme ignorance. Pull the trigger already? Sick fuck? And you have nothing to say? Absolutely nothing left in your heart that would tell you that what happened did not need to turn out that way. But I will promise this. If your knight in shitty armour wants to talk, face to face... I'll show him what sick really means. As for you, I'm sorry it didn't work out, and that we couldn't be civil. I wasted so much time on trying to get over you, so thanks for that extra push. If you hear news that I am dead, know your role. Regret is a bitch.

- XV

Just My Fucking Luck
September 27th, 2013

Somehow I managed to tip my TV over onto my laptop. My beloved laptop. Now the screen is fucked and the only way I can use it is to use the small part that isn't cracked to do shit on. It's expensive to replace the screen, and even more so to replace the computer. Fuck sakes.

Anyway, I have heard that someone is making Facebook pages about my ex (one that charged me). Despite all the negative feelings I have towards her, I feel bad for her. To be publically humiliated hits hard. Maybe she deserves it. I don't know as I have not seen or spoken to her in over 3 years. I hope the police catch whoever it is, and I hope it is who I think it is that is doing that. At least I am not being blamed. I am not that fucking stupid.

Still feel like shit, still abusing (though not as much), and still rotting away in my room. Fuck my life.

- XV

Where The Hell Did I Go?
October 2nd, 2013

Not that anyone reads or even cares. I come to you tonight from my cell, seeing as i dropped a tv on my beloved laptop... RIP.
note to the "infamous" lj friend of mine. Don't let them win. Live, fight, and fucking raise Hell. You can do more alive.

- XV

Drugs Are Bad, Mmmmkayyy?
October 3rd, 2013

Again more drama unfolding before me. I was woken up by a person pissed at another over drugs, of course. And where does that put me? In the middle of a war of sorts. I chose not to pick sides, though that isn't entirely true. Family first, right? It just always seems that I am pulled into other people's shit, as if I don't have enough of my own to deal with. It's stressful and exhausting. I cannot handle it in my current state. I'm so close to the edge, I am worried that a gentle breeze will send me tumbling.

- XV

One of Those Days
October 5th, 2013

I feel really down, and have no energy. Of course feeling like this has the added bonus of increasing my depression exponentially. It's one of those days where I just lay on my bed and listen to music... Marilyn Manson of course, as well as the newly discovered by me electropop band CHVRCHES. Maybe some Butcher Babies to get the anger out of me.

Anyway, though feel better after dealing with a certain situation, i still cannot help the feelings of emptiness that have been increasingly painful lately. I miss Her, I have for years. My patheticness disallows me to move on. I just wish I had someone like Her. Sad, huh?

- XV

Wasting Time
October 10th, 2013

Fuck you too, I'm done trying for nothing. It's pretty obvious when I am the only one getting fucked over and over, what the real issue is.

You don't even know what I would do to you.

- XV

A Long Time Coming
November 19th, 2013

It has been quite a while since my last post, not for lack of stuff to write about. I must say life has improved, with college on the horizon.

-XV

The Lover
November 27th, 2013

He awoke on a bed of dirty linen sheets. The smell of sweat, blood, and human waste filled the small cell. Has it been days? Weeks? With no windows, it seemed like one long, nightmarish day. The sound of footfalls came echoing down the stairs, followed by the jingle of keys and the sound of the cell unlocking. Only a dim candle lit the cell, held by his captor. Even in the flickering light, her pale skin had a hauntingly beautiful aura. It was if the gods had sent an angel to take his life, but first put him through bittersweet torture. In her hand was a 6 inch blade, clearly made for hunting. But this wasn't hunting at all. Her prey stood no chance. As she moves towards him, her beauty paralyzed him. She smiled that perfect smile and grabbed him by the chin, pulling his head back sharply. She placed the knife on his neck, made a 'tsking' sound as she effortlessly slid the blade left to right. His throat opened and his life spilled in spurting bursts. The last thing he was an angel, waiting to take him to the other side.

-XV

Epilogue

So there it is, a year in the life of Me. I understand that what you have read makes little sense, is very twisted, and may even make you question a lot of things; but it is rare that the truth about someone is revealed in such a form. It is a scary thing, getting inside someone's head, especially one who suffers from a mental illness. Even for me, re-reading these posts has opened up old wounds and brought up feelings and memories long forgotten. As I type this, I know that it was a huge risk for me to relive these experiences. It is almost like a totally different person wrote it – and in a way, that is true. I am very different now, but much remains the same. Perhaps the broken man who wrote these posts is still trapped inside. Perhaps the Dark Passenger is lying dormant, waiting for the perfect time to reappear and turn my world upside down.

As I mentioned at the beginning, I have come a long way since these days you have just read about, but I am by no means cured. This will be a life-long battle - a war raging between me and myself, dark and light, right and wrong. Maybe the only difference between now and two years ago is that I am better equipped to deal with the situations that crippled me before. Or maybe it is that my armour is stronger. Maybe things don't get to me like they did before. I don't proclaim to understand my life then, and even now, but I do know that I am no longer as weak and vulnerable as I was when these posts were written.

The question is what now? Do I soldier on as I have since the last entry in this journal, slowly figuring things out and fixing what is broken? Do I assume that the worst is behind me? Is that naïve? There are too many questions to ever be answered, but all I can do is take life day by day, dealing with what comes at me as it happens. Hard lessons were learned, but I made it. I survived.

Finally, I would ask that you reflect on what you have just

read. Did it change your views of mental illness? For better? For worse? Remember that it is a seemingly impossible struggle that millions of people are going through every day. If my words end up helping even one person, saving them from doing the unthinkable, making them realize things CAN get better, then I am happy.

- XV

THE END

Other Works by Topher Edwards:

The BPD Journals II: Remission and Relapse

Coming Soon:

The BPD Journals III

Available on Amazon

Join in the conversation on 'The BPD Journals" Facebook Page

www.facebook.com/thebpdjournals

or watch his videos on YouTube

If you or someone you know is in crisis, please contact your nearest crisis line or suicide support line. They can offer resources and so much more that could save a life.

You are not alone in this. There will always be someone to listen, from family to stranger. Speak up, speak out – end the stigma.

Acknowledgments

I want to thank my mom for never giving up on me, even when I gave up on myself (and her). I also want to thank my brother for being someone I could always look up to. We both had our struggles, but we always had each other's back. Thank you dad for your unconditional support when I needed it the most.

A very special thank you goes to my grandpa, who showed me that no matter how shitty you feel, there is always time for a beer and a laugh. Rest in peace, gramps.

Family is everything - do not take it for granted. In the end, they will be the people fighting by your side.

Other Works by Topher Edwards:

The BPD Journals II: Remission and Relapse

Coming Soon:

The BPD Journals III

Available on Amazon

Join in the conversation on 'The BPD Journals' Facebook Page

www.facebook.com/thebpdjournals

or watch his videos on YouTube

If you or someone you know is in crisis, please contact your nearest crisis line or suicide support line. They can offer resources and so much more that could save a life.

You are not alone in this. There will always be someone to listen, from family to stranger. Speak up, speak out – end the stigma.

- XV